Bariatric A[illegible] Cookbook

1900-Days of Easy, Tasty & Quick Low-Carb Fried Recipes, Including a 30-Day Meal Plan to Guide you After Surgery, and Successfully Keep your Weight Under Control

By
Mary Kane

Table Of Contents

Introduction

In recent years, it has been clear that being overweight significantly increases your risk of acquiring diabetes and other diseases in the future. Losing weight has also been shown to lower sugar levels, which may help to improve or even reverse diabetes in certain people. It has been proven that a drop in body weight may significantly impact your body's insulin resistance and glucose tolerance. However, even if you know these facts and understand that you need to reduce weight, achieving your goals may not be easy. In reality, the weight reduction fight is a lifelong battle that lasts for the rest of their lives for many individuals. This is due to the fact that reducing weight is not always a question of sheer willpower. Rather, there are genuine reasons why some individuals cannot lose weight, no matter how hard they attempt to reduce weight. Bariatric surgery may be the greatest option for persons who are struggling with their weight and have been diagnosed with life-threatening diseases at the same time.

Many obese individuals have benefited from the procedure, which has helped them lose weight and reduce their risk of developing cardiac diseases, diabetes, and premature mortality. There are many distinct forms of bariatric surgery, including gastric bypass. You'll learn more about it in this book. You will see a reduction in glucose levels as a consequence, and the condition of your diabetes will improve. Diabetes is not a condition that can be cured or stopped in its tracks. If your body has a predisposition to insulin resistance, that predisposition will persist indefinitely, and it is also at the heart of the diabetes issue. Even though bariatric surgery may help you lower your sugar levels and eventually stop taking medicines, you will always need to be mindful that if you gain back the weight, diabetes will almost certainly return. The operation is just a highly effective method of controlling the condition and minimizing its potential consequences. Even though this surgery will not completely cure diabetes, if you can maintain a healthy weight, eat well, and exercise regularly, you may be able to live the same life as a non-diabetic with no increased risk factors than if you had never developed the disease. You need to follow a bariatric diet after surgery. This book will teach you all about it. Many healthy recipes are included in this book to help you stay on track.

CHAPTER 1:

Introduction To Bariatric Diet

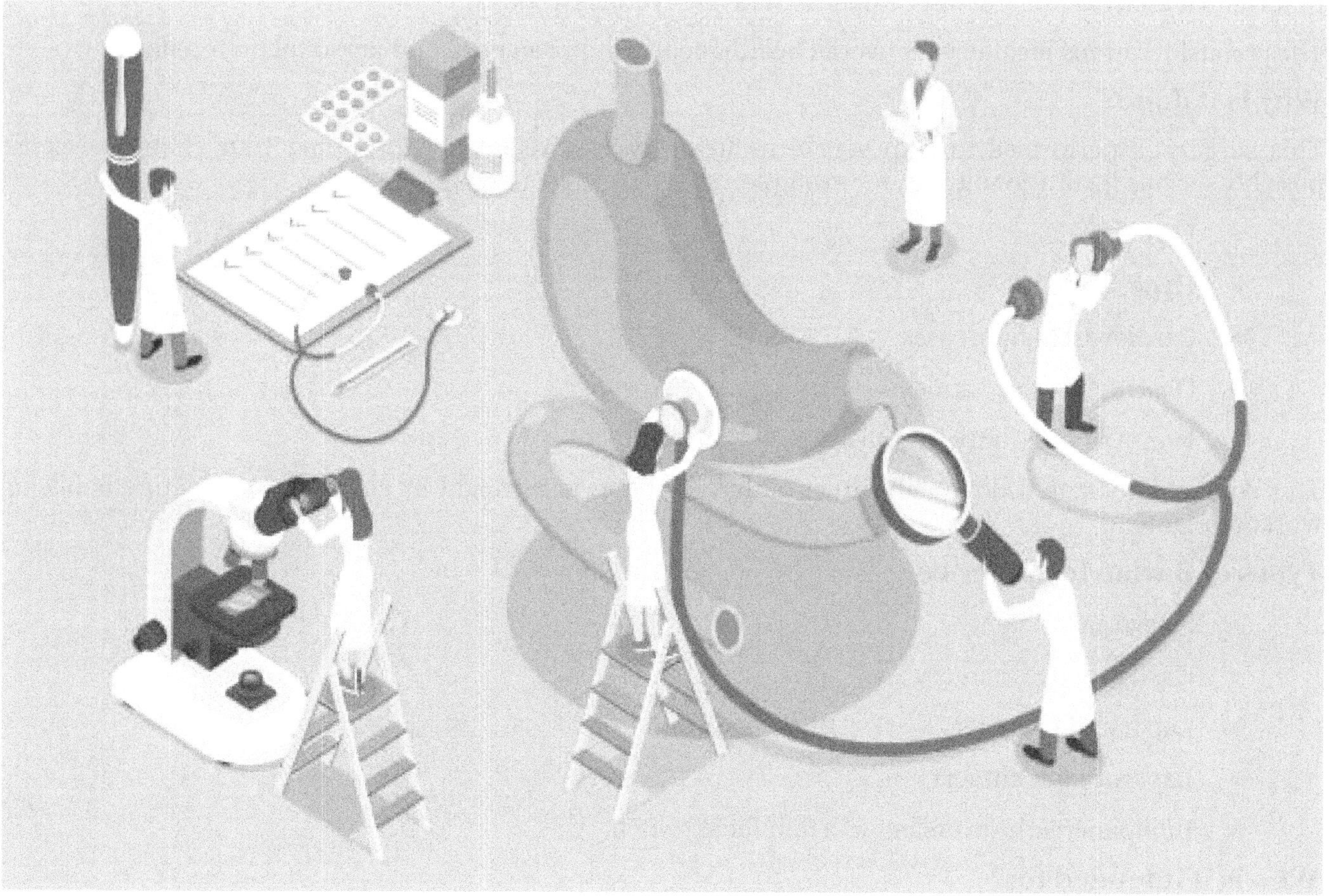

Gastric bypass surgery and some fat loss methods, commonly known as bariatric surgeries, require changing your gastrointestinal system to reduce extra weight.

This surgery is done when exercise and healthy eating have been unsuccessful in reducing your weight or suffering major health problems due to your high BMI.

Some methods have limitations on how much food you can consume.

The efficacy of other procedures is dependent on the body's capacity to digest and absorb different nutrients. Some techniques provide both functions.

1.1 What is Bariatric Surgery?

This surgery is a form of surgery used to help people in reducing weight.

It is a viable option for some overweight individuals and has failed to reduce weight via other means.

If you are severely obese and suffer from an obesity-related health concern, your healthcare professional may recommend that you undergo bariatric surgery.

Diabetes, insomnia, breathing problems, hypertension, and arthritis are just a few of the conditions that might affect you.

With weight reduction, it is possible that diabetes and some other health concerns would improve.

While bariatric surgery has several advantages, it is important to remember that all weight-loss procedures are substantial surgeries that may have significant risks and adverse effects.

Additionally, you must make lasting, healthy modifications to your diet and engage in regular physical activity to help assure the long-term effectiveness of your bariatric surgery procedure.

There are a variety of different bariatric surgery methods available to patients. The kind of bariatric surgery that is most effective for you will be determined by several criteria.

These considerations include your overall health, health requirements, and personal preferences.

Why is it done?

This surgery is performed to help you in reducing excess weight and dropping your chance of getting possibly serious health conditions, for example:

- Diabetes
- Hypertension
- Cardiovascular diseases
- Obstructive sleep apnea
- Non-Alcoholic fatty liver disease

This surgery is normally done only after you have tried to lose weight by changing your eating habits and workout regimen.

Types of Bariatric Surgeries

- Sleeve gastrectomy
- Gastric bypass surgery
- Lap banding surgery
- Laparoscopic surgery
- Biliopancreatic diversion with duodenal switch

Who is it intended for?

In general, this fat-loss surgery may be a possibility for you if you can relate with the following conditions:

- If your BMI is more or equal to 40.
- If your BMI is anywhere between 35 and 39; you are obese.
- If you suffer from a major health problem, such as sleep apnea, type 2 diabetes or hypertension, due to your obesity.
- If it is between 30 and 34 and you suffer from some other health issues, you may be suitable for certain forms of weight-loss procedures in particular circumstances.

This surgery may not be the best choice if you are significantly overweight.

To be considered for this surgery, you may need to fulfill certain requirements. You will very surely be asked to go through a screening procedure to determine your suitability.

It would help if you also were dedicated to making long-standing modifications to live a healthy lifestyle.

In certain cases, patients in follow-up plans may be anticipated to engage in plans that require monitoring their diet, their way of living and conduct, as well as their medical problems.

1.2 Eating Phases of Bariatric Diet

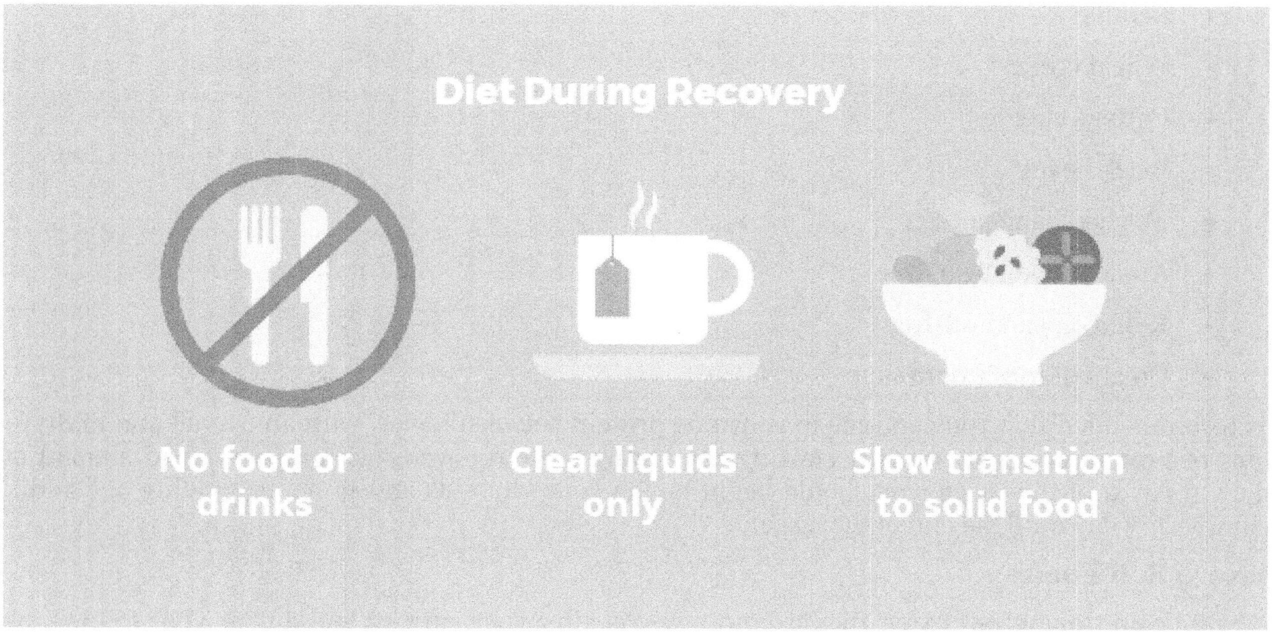

The method of bariatric surgery may be a life-changing experience for people who need to reduce a substantial amount of weight. If you're thinking about having this surgery or have already planned your treatment, it's time to start thinking about how you'll recuperate after the process. The most significant modifications you'll have to make are your eating habits. Following your bariatric surgery, in this section is explained what you should anticipate throughout four major phases of eating following your procedure:

Phase 1: Clear Liquids

You will begin a liquid diet the day following your operation and will continue it for about a week after that. During this period, you should make every effort to increase your fluid intake to around 3 ounces each day, every thirty minutes. Even while this may be tough immediately after your treatment, it will get simpler and more comfortable as time goes on. It is important to drink gently during this period and avoid drinking liquids via a straw or chewing gum since these might cause gas and bloating. Here is a list of clear liquids to have:

- Lemon water
- Lime Gatorade
- Diluted apple juice
- Pedialyte popsicles
- Vegetable broth
- Citrus gelatin, sugar-free
- Protein smoothies

Phase 2: Full Liquids

Generally speaking, you may go to this phase of your diet after around a week, provided that you can handle at least 48 ounces of clear liquids daily. Keep eating every 3 hours, being careful not to miss any meals along the way. A typical serving size for each meal should be 12 cups or two ounces in volume. During this period, you should continue to consume a minimum of 45 to 65 ounces of fluids each day. Foods that you may consume at this period include the following:

- Greek yogurt
- Pea soup

- Oatmeal
- Lentils
- Wheat cream
- Cottage cheese
- Black beans
- Mashed banana
- Apple sauce, sugar-free
- Refined beans, fat-free
- Cream of mushroom soup

It is recommended that you continue to consume protein between meals, with an overall aim of 80 to 100 grams of protein per day. You may start by combining protein powder with unsweetened almond or soy milk. On day 6 of this stage, you should begin taking your vitamins and minerals, adding one additional vitamin every day until the end of the stage.

Phase 3: Soft Foods

You will begin this phase of your diet around 2 weeks after your surgery and during your follow-up visit, and it will run for two full weeks. Each meal should be around 12 cups in size. In any case, even if you have not consumed the recommended quantity, you should stop eating as soon as you feel satisfied. Examples of soft meals that may be consumed at this time include:

- Chicken
- Tofu
- Squash
- Canned tuna
- Avocados
- Zucchini
- Egg whites
- Chickpeas
- Chili
- Salmon
- Cauliflower
- Stew
- Trout
- Peaches
- Refried beans
- Melons
- Mashed lentils
- Mushrooms
- Low-fat cheeses

Between meals, sip fluids as you normally would; however, keep in mind the rule, do not drink for thirty minutes before or after a meal. Continue to drink your regular protein shake and take your daily vitamins and minerals.

Phase 4: Regular Foods

Beginning around 4 to 6 weeks following your operation, you will be required to resume eating ordinary meals. Begin by introducing 1 or 2 new items every day, avoiding foods that induce gas, such as broccoli, onions, spicy meals, peppers, and gradually increasing your intake. Eat slowly and thoroughly before swallowing and remember to chew your meal entirely before swallowing.

It is recommended that each meal be around 6 ounces in size and not exceed 1 cup. You should continue to adhere to the guidelines. You will eventually be able to transition to a normal diet; however, there are particular items that you should avoid for the time being:

- Rice
- Oils
- Added sugars
- Pasta
- Dry meats
- Bread
- Fried foods
- Alcohol
- Baked goods
- Carbonated drinks
- Fruit with thick skin

1.3 Diet Tips After Bariatric Surgery

You will have to follow the bariatric diet for the rest of your life. Your daily diet will consist of three modest meals and eight ounces of fat-free milk for snacks, which you will have three times each day. If you want to start a bariatric diet, here are some tips for you:

- Consume water in large quantities, at least 6 to 8 glasses per day. Avoid drinking for thirty minutes before and after eating a meal.
- Protein should be consumed first, followed by carbs.
- For the first four months after your operation, refrain from consuming rough or gristly red meat. It is safe to consume if the beef has been cooked in a slow cooker for many hours.
- For the first four months, refrain from eating white bread.
- Consume healthy foods such as baked, grilled, steamed, or broiled dishes to maintain a healthy weight. Foods that are fried should be avoided.
- Take vitamin and mineral supplements as directed by your physician.
- Follow all the post-surgery rules, including follow-up appointments, exercise, dietary guidelines, etc.
- Continue to engage in strength and aerobic activity for a minimum of 30 to 50 minutes every day.
- Increase the diversity and intensity of your workout with time.

1.4 How to Get Started with the Bariatric Diet?

Following bariatric surgery, you must adhere to the dietary recommendations that have been provided to you. The purpose of these recommendations, developed with care by your healthcare specialists, is to keep you from overindulging in calories while also providing you with balanced meals that help avoid nutritional shortages and retain muscle tissue.

Although this new eating style may seem daunting at first, most patients find that the recommendations become a part of their daily routine over some time.

General Instructions

- Balanced meals should be consumed in modest quantities.
- Consume a diet that is low in calories, fat, and sugar.
- Slowly chew little pieces of food until they are fully chewed.
- It is recommended that you consume between 350 and 600 calories per day for the first two months after surgery.
- Record your daily meal quantities, as well as your calorie and protein consumption.
- The daily caloric intake should not be more than 1000 calories per day.

What to Avoid?

- Avoid caffeine.
- Sugar-containing meals and drinks, concentrated sweets, and juices should be avoided at all costs.
- It is best to avoid grains, bread, raw veggies, fresh fruits, and meats that are difficult to chew, such as pig and steak.
- The use of straws, fizzy drinks, and ice chewing is prohibited. They have the potential to bring air into your gastric pouch, causing pain.

- Don't use alcoholic drinks of any kind. After surgery, alcohol is taken into your system considerably more rapidly than it was before, making its sedative and mood-altering effects more difficult to anticipate and regulate than they were before the procedure.

Fluids Intake

- To prevent dehydration, drink plenty of water and calorie-free drinks between meals.
- Drink around 1 cup of liquids five to eight times a day between each small meal.
- Drink at least 2 liters of fluids every day to keep your body hydrated. You will be able to fulfill this goal in stages throughout time.

Protein Intake

Consume meals high in protein to help keep muscular tissue in good condition. The following foods include high Proteins:

- Fish
- Eggs
- Tuna
- Meat
- Tofu
- Seafood
- Yogurt
- Soy milk
- Cottage cheese

Your daily protein intake should be between at least 65 grams, at the very least. Don't be concerned if you cannot achieve this target during the first several months after bariatric surgery.

Supplements

You must take the supplements listed below daily to avoid vitamin shortages from occurring.

All tablets must be broken or cut into little pieces, as specified by the manufacturer.

Your ability to absorb entire tablets is reduced compared to before surgery, and it may be difficult for pills to pass through your newly formed anatomy after bariatric surgery.

Multivitamins

Consume a daily chewable multivitamin and mineral supplement with iron, copper, folic acid, selenium and zinc at a concentration of 400 mcg per serving.

If you had bariatric surgery, you should take two pills daily for at least three months and then one tablet daily for the rest of your life.

Vitamin B12

Take 500 mg every day. It may be taken orally as a tablet or sublingually, which means it can be ingested beneath the tongue.

Calcium

Take 1,200 to 2,000 mg daily to avoid calcium shortage and osteoporosis.

Take the calcium in two separate doses throughout the day to maximize absorption.

Vitamin D

Take it twice a day in split doses of 500 IUs. It is recommended that you take your calcium supplement with vitamin D. If you want to avoid taking numerous tablets, you may take a combined supplement, as long as it provides the appropriate amounts of both nutrients.

1.5 How to Use Air Fryer in Bariatric Diet and its Advantages?

Firstly, using an air fryer enables us to create crispy dishes comparable in flavor to deep-fried items but without needing to use as much oil as deep-frying does. It certainly seems like a victory, but is it beneficial to one's health?

To begin, let us discuss how the air fryer truly works. It is equipped with a fry basket that enables food to be hung and exposed to heat from all sides, ideal for crisping up foods. The difference is that instead of being immersed in hot oil, the food is exposed to very hot, rotating air, similar to what happens in an oven.

So, now that we've covered the basics of how the air fryer works, let's talk about how it is good for bariatric patients. Such patients need to have fat-free and healthy foods, and an air fryer is the best appliance for it. It saves time and also helps in making healthy foods.

Advantages

Several studies have shown that air-frying chicken may reduce the quantity of fatty acids in the fish while simultaneously increasing the number of inflammatory chemicals in the fish's flesh. However, it is crucial to remember that each time a meal is subjected to heat, its composition will alter, and inflammatory chemicals may arise due to this exposure. The same research discovered that cooking chicken with anti-inflammatory herbs might assist in lessening fat oxidation that occurs when it is air-fried. While there is a possibility that the high temperatures produced by the air fryer would expedite these processes, additional study is required to discover if this is the case.

When comparing the results of deep-frying, there is a clear winner. Air frying is preferable for many reasons, the most important of which is the reduced quantity of oil utilized. In contrast to the deep fryer, which needs many liters of oil, the air fryer requires none. This is a positive for the air fryer since using less oil typically consumes fewer calories, lowering the likelihood of gaining weight or becoming obese. Hence it is best for bariatric patients.

Chronic diseases, such as cardiac diseases, are less likely to occur due to these dietary changes. Depending on the kind of oil used, consuming less oil may also result in a lower intake of saturated fat, contributing to a lower risk of developing cardiac diseases in the long run.

The air fryer is generally considered a better alternative since it contains fewer calories and may result in less inflammation, thereby lowering the chance of developing chronic illness in the long run.

Air fryers are helpful for bariatric patients, and it enables them to follow a bariatric diet easily. In contrast, the true determinant is the kind of foods you consume and place in the air fryer. Foods high in nutrients are typically just as healthy when cooked in an air fryer as in the oven.

CHAPTER 2:

Breakfast Recipes

1. Quiche

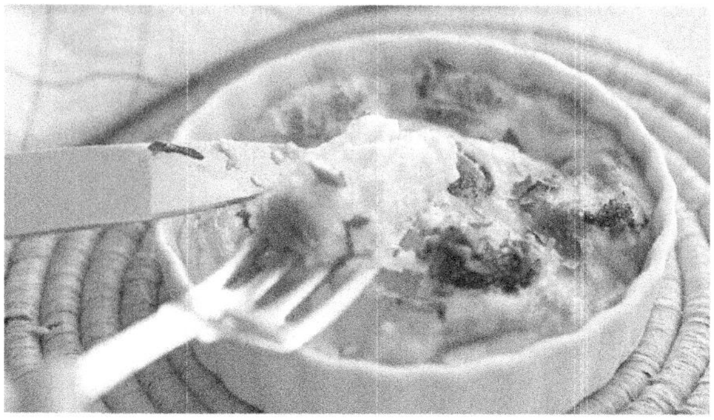

Prep time: 10 minutes

Cook time: 15 minutes

Servings: 4

Ingredients

- 3 eggs
- Olive oil spray
- 2 tbsp of whole milk
- 1/4 tsp of salt
- 1/4 tsp of thyme
- 1/8 tsp of pepper
- 1/4 bell pepper, chopped
- 2 tbsp of low-fat cheese
- 1/4 cup of onions, chopped
- 3 grape tomatoes, cut into halves

Instructions

Preheat the air fryer to 360°F for about 5 minutes. In a large mixing bowl, mix all the ingredients. Then use a nonstick spray and spray it onto a pan. After that, pour in the mixture. Cook for about 8 minutes, turning halfway during the entire cooking time. Let it cool and then serve.

Nutrients: Kcal 93, Fats: 6g, Total Carbs: 3g, Proteins: 7g

2. Apple Fritters

Prep time: 10 minutes

Cook time: 12 minutes

Servings: 10

Ingredients

- Glaze
- 2 eggs
- 1/2 tsp of salt
- 1/4 cup of butter
- 2 tsp of vanilla extract
- 1/4 cup of brown sugar
- 1.5 tsp of cinnamon
- 2/3 cup of whole milk
- 2 tsp of baking powder
- 1.5 cups of almond flour
- 1 cup of powdered brown sugar
- 2 cups of apples, sliced

Instructions

Preheat the air fryer to 400°F for around 5 minutes. Combine the dry ingredients in a mixing bowl. Add whole milk, eggs and vanilla extract to another bowl. Combine all of the ingredients to form a batter. Fold in apples in the mixture. Scoop the batter and pour it into the baking basket. Cook for about 7 minutes. To make the glaze, melt the butter in a pan. Set aside to cool before mixing the powdered brown sugar and whole milk to thin it down. Pour it over fritters and enjoy.

Nutrients: Kcal 215, Fats: 6g, Total Carbs: 36g, Proteins: 4g

3. Sweet Potato Cubes

Prep time: 10 minutes

Cook time: 15 minutes

Servings: 6

Ingredients

- 1/4 cup of honey
- 3-4 tbsp of olive oil
- 2 tbsp of cinnamon
- 2-3 sweet potatoes
- 1/2 cup of brown sugar

Instructions

Preheat the air fryer to 350°F for about 5 minutes. Toss the sweet potatoes in a basin with olive oil until they are well covered. Toss in the cinnamon and sugar before drizzling on the honey. Spray the air fryer basket. Cook at 350°F for about 20 minutes. When serving, pour a little extra honey on top.Nutrients: Kcal 246, Fats: 7g, Total Carbs: 47g, Proteins: 1g

4. Zucchini Bread

Prep time: 10 minutes

Cook time: 35 minutes

Servings: 12

Ingredients

- 2 eggs
- 1 tsp of vanilla
- 1/2 tsp of salt
- 2 cups of zucchini
- 1/2 cup of vegetable oil
- 1 cup of brown sugar
- 1/2 tsp of baking soda
- 1/2 tsp of cinnamon
- 1/2 tsp of baking powder
- 1/4 tsp of nutmeg
- 1.5 cups of almond flour

Instructions

In a small bowl, combine all of the dry items. Whisk together the eggs, vanilla extract, brown sugar, and oil in a separate dish. Slowly integrate the dry ingredients into the batter until well combined. Then fold in the grated zucchini with care. Use a nonstick spray to coat two loaf pans. After 5 minutes of preheating, add the loaves and bake them for about 35 minutes at 310°F in the air fryer. Serve and enjoy.

Nutrients: Kcal 215, Fats: 10g, Total Carbs: 29g, Proteins: 3g

5. Egg Rolls

Prep time: 10 minutes

Cook time: 15 minutes

Servings: 4

Ingredients

For Roll Filling

- 1/4 cabbage
- 2 tsp of sesame oil
- 2 tbsp of soy sauce
- 2 tsp of ginger, grated
- 2 tbsp of rice vinegar
- 2 green onions, chopped
- 2 tsp of chili paste
- 1 carrot, sliced

For the Sauce

- 2 tbsp of honey
- 2 tsp of soy sauce
- 1 tsp of ginger, grated
- 2 tsp of rice vinegar
- 1 tsp of pepper paste
- 1 tsp of spicy mustard

For the Egg Roll

- 1 tbsp of olive oil
- 4 roll wrappers
- 1 egg, beaten

Instructions

Mix all the roll-filling ingredients in a bowl. Saute the mixture in a pan for about 3 minutes. Preheat the air fryer for about 10 minutes at 390°F. Fill the roll wrapper with the mixture, brush the edges with egg, and roll-up. Cook for 15 minutes, turning every 3 minutes. Combine all of the mentioned sauce ingredients in a bowl to make the sauce. Serve egg rolls with dipping sauce.

Nutrients: Kcal 198, Fats: 9g, Total Carbs: 22g, Proteins: 6g

6. Chicken Omelet

Prep time: 10 minutes

Cook time: 15 minutes

Servings: 2

Ingredients

- 4 eggs - 1/2 tsp of salt
- 1/2 cup of Tyson - 1/4 tsp of black pepper
- Grilled chicken breast 2 tbsp of shredded cheese - 1/4 tsp of garlic, chopped
- 1/4 tsp of onion powder

Instructions

Spray ramekins with olive oil. Fill each ramekin halfway with eggs. Sprinkle the grated cheese, chicken, and spices on top. Cook for about 14 minutes at 330°F. Serve and enjoy.

Nutrients: Kcal 270, Fats: 6g, Total Carbs: 12g, Proteins: 21g

7. Breakfast Burrito

Prep time: 10 minutes

Cook time: 35 minutes

Servings: 10

Ingredients

- 10 eggs
- 1 tsp of olive oil - 2 tsp of sea salt
- 1 tsp of black pepper
- 3 cups of cheese, shredded
- 10 pieces of flour tortillas
- 2 cups of russet potato
- 1 pound of breakfast sausage

Instructions

Scramble eggs in a pan. Place the potatoes and sausage in the air fryer. Cook at 325°F for about 20 minutes. After 15 minutes of cooking, remove the foil and continue cooking for 5 more minutes. Spread the mixture on tortillas and wrap them up. Top the burritos with cheese. Serve and enjoy.

Nutrients: Kcal 317, Fats: 24g, Total Carbs: 4g, Proteins: 19g

8. French Toast Sticks

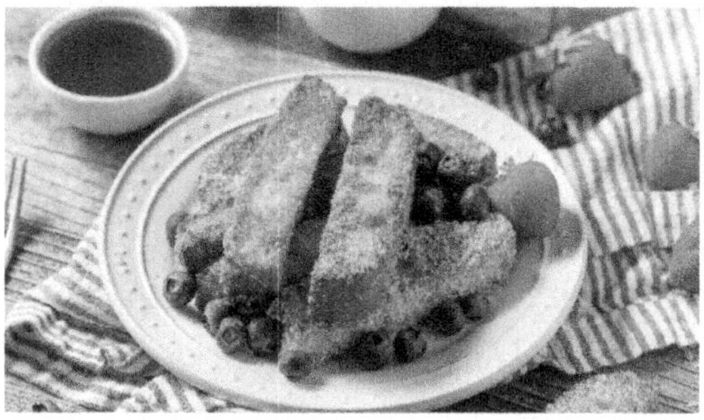

Prep time: 10 minutes

Cook time: 5 minutes

Servings: 10

Ingredients

- Cinnamon powder - 3 large eggs
- 1/3 cup of coconut milk
- 1 loaf of challah bread
- 1/3 cup of coconut sugar

Instructions

Slice the bread into sticks. Spray the coconut oil to coat the basket of the air fryer. Whisk in the eggs, coconut sugar, and whole milk until well combined. Dip the sticks into the mixture, covering both sides of the bread. Place the sticks in an air fryer basket and sprinkle with cinnamon powder. Cook for about 5 minutes at 380°F in the air fryer. If preferred, serve with maple syrup.

Nutrients: Kcal 40, Fats: 0.7g, Total Carbs: 6.7g, Proteins: 1.5g

9. Cinnamon Rolls

Prep time: 10 minutes

Cook time: 35 minutes

Servings: 10

Ingredients

- 2 tbsp of brown sugar
- 1/4 cup of raisins
- 1/3 cup of nuts, chopped
- 1 tbsp of cinnamon powder
- 1/3 cup of coconut sugar
- 2 tbsp of maple syrup
- 1/3 cup of butter, melted
- 1 pack of crescent roll

Instructions

Combine the melted butter, brown sugar, and maple syrup in a large mixing bowl. Fill the pan of the air fryer halfway with the mixture. Sprinkle the nuts and raisins onto the pan and set them aside. Combine the cinnamon powder and coconut sugar; dip each roll piece into the mixture. Then, place each one on your pan on top of your mixture and cook for about 35 minutes at 345°F. Serve and enjoy.

Nutrients: Kcal 143, Fats: 8g, Total Carbs: 17g, Proteins: 1g

10. Apple Crisps

Prep time: 10 minutes

Cook time: 25 minutes

Servings: 10

Ingredients

- 1 tbsp of brown sugar
- 1/4 cup of oats
- 1/2 cup of almond flour
- 1/8 of nutmeg
- 1/2 cup of coconut sugar
- 1/4 tsp of cinnamon powder
- 2 tbsp of all-purpose flour
- 4 tbsp of butter
- 1 tbsp of apple cider vinegar
- 2 apples, sliced
- 1/4 cup of raisins or cranberries

Instructions

Add the mentioned ingredients except for butter, oats, brown sugar, cinnamon, flour and mix it until well combined. At this point, you can add raisins or cranberries to it. Divide the ingredients evenly into cups and pour apple cider vinegar on top. Preheat the air fryer for about 4 minutes at 350°F. Combine the remaining ingredients in a separate bowl. Cover the cups with foil after spooning this equally over the tops. Cook for another 16 minutes. If desired, top with ice cream or caramel syrup.

Nutrients: Kcal 718, Fats: 49g, Total Carbs: 321g, Proteins: 13g

11. Breakfast Bagels

Prep time: 10 minutes

Cook time: 15 minutes

Servings: 4

Ingredients

- 1 cup of Greek yogurt
- 1 cup of self-rising flour
- 2 tbsp of cinnamon powder
- 2 tbsp of brown sugar
- 1/2 cup of cream cheese, whipped

Instructions

Combine the flour and yogurt in a mixing bowl and make dough. Spray pan with nonstick cooking spray. Form dough into balls and put them in a frying basket. Sprinkle bagels with cinnamon and brown sugar. Set the air fryer to 325°F and cook for about 15 minutes. Let them cool fully before filling with cream cheese. Serve and enjoy.

Nutrients: Kcal 657, Fats: 32 g, Total Carbs: 96g, Proteins: 35g

12. Healthy Chocolate Oats

Prep time: 10 minutes

Cook time: 5 minutes

Servings: 4

Ingredients

- Chocolate chips
- Strawberries
- 2 cups of quick oats
- 1/2 cup of dark chocolate
- 4 cups of chocolate almond milk

Instructions

Add the oats and chocolate almond milk together in a dish. Pour water and this mixture into the air fryer basket. Cook for about 5 minutes at 350°F. Top with chocolate chips and strawberries. Serve and enjoy.

Nutrients: Kcal 296, Fats: 11 g, Total Carbs: 43g, Proteins: 7g

13. Hash Browns

Prep time: 10 minutes

Cook time: 25 minutes

Servings: 6

Ingredients

- 1 tsp of salt
- 1/2 tsp of black pepper
- 1 onion, chopped
- 1 cup of cheese, shredded
- 4 potatoes

Instructions

Mix the potatoes, pepper, onions, and salt in a bowl. Add the mixture to a greased air fryer basket. Cook for about 20 minutes at 400°F. If desired, top with cheese and cook for 3 minutes until the cheese is melted.

Nutrients: Kcal 84, Fats: 6 g, Total Carbs: 2g, Proteins: 5g

14. Stuffed Peppers

Prep time: 10 minutes

Cook time: 15 minutes

Servings: 2

Ingredients

- 4 eggs
- 2 bell peppers
- 1 tsp of olive oil
- 1 pinch of chili flakes
- 1 pinch of salt and pepper

Instructions

Spray oil over bell pepper. Crack eggs into each bell pepper. Season them with spices. Cook for about 13 minutes at 390°F in the air fryer. Serve and enjoy.

Nutrients: Kcal 164, Fats: 10 g, Total Carbs: 4g, Proteins: 11g

15. Sausage Patties

Prep time: 10 minutes

Cook time: 10 minutes

Servings: 8

Ingredients

- 2 eggs
- 8 sausage patties
- Olive oil spray

Instructions

Preheat the air fryer for 5 minutes at 400°F. Spray the basket with olive oil spray. If you want to put an egg in each silicone cup, you may do so at this point. Cook the sausage for about 7 minutes, turning halfway through. Cook the eggs for 5 minutes, take them from the air fryer basket, and rest in the cups for 3 minutes. Serve and enjoy.

Nutrients: Kcal 65, Fats: 6 g, Total Carbs: 2g, Proteins: 3g

16. Avocado Salad Bowl

Prep time: 10 minutes

Cook time: 20 minutes

Servings: 4

Ingredients

- 2 tbsp pesto
- 1 cup of romaine lettuce
- 1 avocado, diced
- 4 oz. of fresh mozzarella
- 1 cup of cherry tomatoes
- 0.56 lb of skinless and boneless chicken
- 2 tbsp balsamic vinaigrette

Instructions

Add broth, chicken, and pesto to the air fryer basket. Cook for about 10 minutes at 390°F. Once it is cooked, set it aside to cool. Shred-it later. Add all the other ingredients in a bowl along with the shredded chicken. Sprinkle vinaigrette on top. Serve and enjoy.

Nutrients: Kcal: 258, Total Carbs: 8g, Proteins: 25g, Fats: 14g

17. Avocado Egg Boats

Prep time: 10 minutes

Cook time: 10 minutes

Servings: 2

Ingredients

- Salt
- Pepper
- Chives
- 4 eggs
- Parsley
- 2 avocados

Instructions

Cut avocados in half. For seasoning them, use chives, salt, parsley, and pepper. In each half, crack an egg, put it in the air fryer, and cook for about 8 minutes at 275°F. Serve and enjoy.

Nutrients: Kcal 447, Fats: 38g, Total Carbs: 18g, Proteins: 15g

18. Stuffed Mushrooms

Prep time: 10 minutes

Cook time: 10 minutes

Servings: 2

Ingredients

- Salt and pepper
- 2 tsp of minced garlic
- 1/3 cup of olive oil
- 1 cup of white mushrooms
- 2 tbsp of minced parsley
- 1/2 cup of breadcrumbs
- 1/2 cup of low-fat cheese, grated

Instructions

Mix everything in a bowl. Stuff mushrooms with the mixture. Place the mushrooms in a greased air fryer basket. Cook at 340°F for about 8 minutes. Plate, serve and enjoy.

Nutrients: Kcal 51, Fats: 4g, Total Carbs: 3g, Proteins: 1g

19. Sweet Bacon

Prep time: 10 minutes

Cook time: 10 minutes

Servings: 2

Ingredients

- 1 lb of bacon
- 1/4 cup of brown sugar
- 1 to 2 tsp of black pepper

Instructions

Begin by preheating the air fryer for 5 minutes at 390°F. After that, rub the bacon with brown sugar and season with black pepper. Cook for about 8 minutes. Cook until it reaches your desired crispiness. Serve and enjoy.

Nutrients: Kcal 577, Fats: 40g, Total Carbs: 14g, Proteins: 39g

20. Strawberry Pop-Tarts

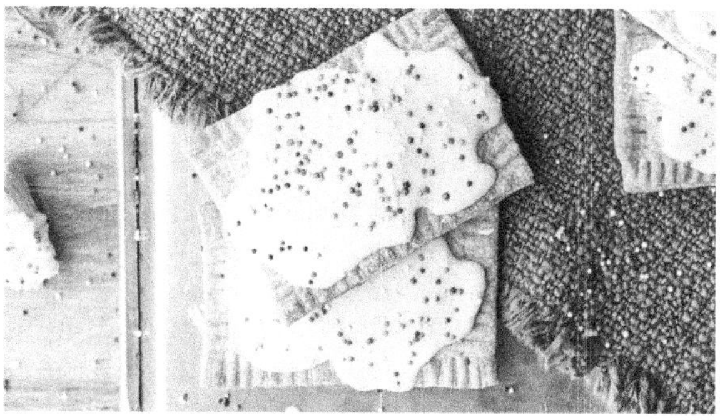

Prep time: 10 minutes

Cook time: 15 minutes

Servings: 8

Ingredients

- 2 tbsp of whole milk
- 1 egg
- 15 oz of pie crusts
- 1 cup of powdered brown sugar
- 5 ounces of strawberry jelly

Instructions

Cut pie crust into circles. Place jelly in the center. Brush the edges with egg wash. Cover with another pie circle and jelly. Cook at 370°F for about 12 minutes. Transfer to a cooling rack after removing from the air fryer. To make the icing, whisk the powdered brown sugar and whole milk in a small bowl until it reaches the appropriate consistency. Enjoy pop tarts with this icing.

Nutrients: Kcal 229, Fats: 9g, Total Carbs: 39g, Proteins: 2g

21. Blueberry Crisps

Prep time: 10 minutes

Cook time: 15 minutes

Servings: 2

Ingredients

- 1 pinch of salt
- 1 tsp of lemon juice
- 1 1/2 tbsp of brown sugar
- 1 cup of frozen blueberries
- 2 tsp of all-purpose flour
- 1/2 tsp of cinnamon powder
- 3 tbsp of quick oats
- 1 1/2 tbsp of unsalted butter

Instructions

Preheat the air fryer at 360°F. Mix berries, salt, lemon juice, and flour in a bowl. Add all the remaining ingredients to another bowl to make the topping mixture. Cover berry mixture with this and cook in the air fryer for about 14 minutes. Take it out once it is done and enjoy.

Nutrients: Kcal 217, Fats: 9.7g, Total Carbs: 31.8g, Proteins: 2.3g

22. Egg Sandwich

Prep time: 10 minutes

Cook time: 10 minutes

Servings: 2

Ingredients

- Salt
- 1 bagel
- 1 deli ham
- Black pepper
- 1 egg
- Low-fat cheese

Instructions

Toast bagel in the air fryer for about 3 minutes at 320°F. Fry egg in a pan. Season it with salt and pepper. Put egg, deli ham on top of toasted bagel and sprinkle cheese over it. Wrap in aluminum foil and put it in the air fryer for about 3 minutes at 340°F. Serve and enjoy.

Nutrients: Kcal 511, Fats: 19g, Total Carbs: 58g, Proteins: 28g

CHAPTER 3:

Lunch Recipes

1. Tasty Tacos

Prep time: 10 minutes

Cook time: 20 minutes

Servings: 4

Ingredients

- 12 corn taco shells
- 1 lb of ground turkey
- Shredded lettuce
- 1 pack of gluten-free taco seasoning
- 1 cup of Black beans
- 1/2 cup of Shredded low-fat cheese
- 2 Tomatoes, chopped

Instructions

Cook turkey in pan. Then add seasoning and other stuff to the taco. Add the tacos to the air fryer. Cook on 355°F till crispy. Serve and enjoy!

Nutrition: Kcal: 237, Fats: 2g, Total Carbs: 20g, Proteins: 20g

2. Fajitas

Prep time: 5 minutes

Cook time: 15 minutes

Servings: 8

Ingredients

- 2 boneless chicken breasts, sliced
- 3 bell peppers
- 1 onion, chopped
- 3 tbsp of fajita seasoning
- 1 tbsp of vegetable oil

Instructions

Preheat the air fryer to 390°F. Season the chicken. Put everything in the air fryer cook for about 15 minutes, tossing midway through. Serve and enjoy.

Nutrition: Kcal: 154, Fats: 10g, Total Carbs: 4g, Proteins: 11g

3. Garlic Mushrooms

Prep time: 10 minutes

Cook time: 15 minutes

Servings: 2

Ingredients

- 8 oz. of dried mushrooms
- 2 tbsp of olive oil
- 1 tbsp of garlic powder
- 1 tsp of soy sauce
- Salt for taste
- Pepper for taste
- 1 tbsp of chopped parsley

Instructions

Cut mushrooms equally. Add to the bowl, then toss with garlic powder, oil, soy sauce, black pepper, and salt. Cook at 380°F, flipping and shaking midway. Squeeze lemon juice. Serve warm.

Nutrition: Kcal: 92, Fats: 7g, Total Carbs: 4g, Proteins: 3g

4. Zucchini Fries

Prep time: 15 minutes

Cook time: 25 minutes

Servings: 6

Ingredients

- 2 zucchinis, sliced
- 1 egg
- 1/3 tsp of salt
- 1 cup of almond flour
- 1/2 cup of low-fat cheese
- 1 tsp of garlic powder
- 1 tsp of Italian herbs

Instructions

Preheat the air fryer at 425°F and line the pan with parchment paper. In a small basin, softly whisk the egg with the salt. Mix the almond flour, cheese, garlic, and herbs in a second bowl. Dip zucchini fries in the egg wash, then transfer to the dry mixture. Put in a flat layer on the baking sheet. Cook for about 30 minutes, turning midway. Serve.

Nutrition: Kcal: 168, Fats: 2g, Total Carbs: 8g, Proteins: 8g

5. Salmon Fillets

Prep time: 2 minutes

Cook time: 8 minutes

Servings: 4

Ingredients

- 4 salmon fillets
- 1 tbsp of olive oil
- 1 tbsp of garlic powder
- 1/2 tbsp of paprika
- Salt and pepper for taste
- Lemon
- Tartar serving

Instructions

Preheat the air fryer to 400°F. Rub each fillet with olive oil and season with spices. Place the salmon in the air fryer and cook for about 9 minutes. Serve and enjoy.

Nutrition: Kcal: 276, Fats: 14g, Total Carbs: 1g, Proteins: 34g

6. Shrimps

Prep time: 5 minutes

Cook time: 10 minutes

Servings: 4

Ingredients

- 2/3 cup of almond flour
- 4 eggs
- 1 tbsp of black pepper
- 1 tsp of smoked paprika
- 1 tsp of lemon pepper
- 20 peeled and deveined large shrimps

Instructions

Preheat the air fryer at 390°F. Mix everything in a bowl except eggs. In another bowl, beat the eggs. Dip the shrimps in the egg mixture, then dip it in the flour mixture. Place the shrimps in a single layer in the air fryer basket and cook for about 12 minutes at 390°F. Serve when golden brown.

Nutrition: Kcal: 98, Fats: 6g, Total Carbs: 1g, Proteins: 8g

7. Kale Chips

Prep time: 5 minutes

Cook time: 10 minutes

Servings: 4

Ingredients

- 11 oz of fresh kale
- 1 tbsp of olive oil
- 1/2 cup of grated low-fat cheese
- Pepper and salt for taste

Instructions

Add the kale and olive oil to a bowl, and season with salt and pepper. For about 5 minutes, air fry the kale at 270°F. Sprinkle cheese on the chips. Cook for another 2 minutes. Serve and enjoy!

Nutrition: Kcal: 60, Fats: 2g, Total Carbs: 3g, Proteins: 3g

8. Parmesan Broccoli

Prep time: 5 minutes

Cook time: 5 minutes

Servings: 4

Ingredients

- 2 broccolis
- 4 tbsp of melted butter
- 2 cloves of minced garlic
- 1/2 cup of Parmesan cheese, grated
- 1 tsp of red pepper flakes
- Black pepper and salt for taste

Instructions

Preheat the air fryer to 400°F. Set aside the broccoli florets. Combine and mix all the ingredients in a bowl. Cook the broccoli for about 6 minutes in the air fryer, shake the basket in midway. Serve broccoli with some parmesan cheese sprinkled over it.

Nutrition: Kcal: 87, Fats: 1g, Total Carbs: 20g, Proteins: 2g

9. Meaty Burger Bites

Prep time: 15 minutes

Cook time: 30 minutes

Servings: 4

Ingredients

- 1.5 lbs of beef
- 3 oz of minced raw bacon
- 2 tbsp of yellow mustard
- 1/2 tsp of salt - 1/2 tsp of onion powder
- 1/4 tsp of black pepper
- 1 lettuce
- 3 cherry tomatoes
- 3 jalapenos, thinly sliced
- 3 sliced pickles

Instructions

Mix everything in a bowl. Make small balls. Preheat the air fryer to 400°F. Lay these in a single layer. Cook, turning halfway through until done to your liking, about 10 minutes for medium. Serve with any sauce and enjoy.

Nutrition: Kcal: 120, Fats: 6g, Total Carbs: 2g, Proteins: 14g

10. Crispy Chicken Thighs

Prep time: 5 minutes

Cook time: 20 minutes

Servings: 4

Ingredients

- 4 chicken thighs with skin
- 1/2 tsp of kosher salt
- 1 tsp of smoked paprika
- 1 tsp of garlic powder
- 1/2 tsp of oregano
- 1/2 tsp of onion powder

Instructions

Start with preheating the air fryer for about 5 minutes at 380°F. Season chicken with all the seasoning. Cook in the air fryer for 15 minutes, flipping after every 5 minutes, making sure all the sides are well cooked. Serve and enjoy!

Nutrition: Kcal: 237, Fats: 2g, Total Carbs: 20g, Proteins: 20g

11. Tuna Steak

Prep time: 5 minutes

Cook time: 4 minutes

Servings: 4

Ingredients

- 8 oz of tuna steaks
- 3 tbsp of olive oil
- 2 tsp of the desired seasoning
- 1 tsp of garlic powder and pepper

For Tomato Paste

- 2 celery stalks

- 4 scallions
- 2 yellow bell peppers
- 1 cup of tomatoes
- 2 tbsp of sugar
- 2 tbsp of white wine
- 1/2 tsp of crushed red pepper flakes

Instructions

Preheat the air fryer for 4 minutes at 375°F. Take a small bowl and combine all seasonings. Coat all sides of the tuna with olive oil and spices. Fry the tuna for 2 minutes before flipping it over. Allow the tuna to settle for 2 minutes before serving with the lemon and tomato paste.

Nutrition: Kcal: 237, Fats: 7g, Total Carbs: 7g, Proteins: 44g

12. Chicken With Veggies

Prep time: 10 minutes

Cook time: 20 minutes

Servings: 4

Ingredients

- 1 lb of chicken breast
- 1 cup of broccoli
- 1 chopped zucchini
- 1 cup of chopped bell peppers
- 1 chopped onion
- 2 cloves of crushed garlic
- 2 tbsp of olive oil
- 1 tsp of chili powder
- 1 tsp of garlic powder
- 1 tsp of salt and pepper
- 1 tbsp of Italian seasoning

Instructions

Preheat the air fryer to 400°F. Add the chopped vegetables and chicken to a large mixing bowl. Toss the oil and spices into it. Cook in the air fryer for about 15 minutes. Serve and enjoy.

Nutrition: Kcal: 237, Fats: 5g, Total Carbs: 8g, Proteins: 26g

13. Cheesy Chicken

Prep time: 10 minutes

Cook time: 20 minutes

Servings: 4

Ingredients

- 4 oz of chicken breast
- 1 cup of grated parmesan cheese
- 3 tbsp of marinara sauce
- 3 large eggs
- 1 cup of shredded low-fat cheese
- 1/4 tsp garlic onion powder
- 1/2 tsp of pepper and salt

Instructions

Mix everything in a bowl except for the eggs and the chicken. Whisk eggs in another bowl. Dip the chicken breast in the egg wash, then in the other mixture. Cook for around 10 minutes at 380°F. Flip over and top with marinara sauce and cheese. Cook for another 6 minutes. Serve and enjoy.

Nutrition: Kcal: 337, Fats: 2g, Total Carbs: 10g, Proteins: 30g

14. Chicken Patties

Prep time: 10 minutes

Cook time: 12 minutes

Servings: 4

Ingredients

- 1 egg
- 1 tbsp of dill
- 2 oz of pork rinds
- 1/2 tsp of garlic powder
- 1 tsp of salt

- 1 tsp of pepper
- 3 chopped green onions
- 1/4 tsp of onion powder
- 1 lb of ground chicken thigh meat
- 1/2 cup of shredded low-fat cheese
- 1/2 cup of shredded Provolone

Instructions

Combine the ground chicken, low-fat cheese, onions, garlic powder, and onion powder in a large mixing bowl. Make patties. Place the patties in the refrigerator. In a medium bowl, whisk the egg. In another bowl, combine the ground rinds and dill. Dip each one into the egg mixture, then press the pork rinds to coat completely. Fill the air fryer basket halfway with patties. Cook at 360°F for about 12 minutes. Serve and enjoy!

Nutrition: Kcal: 304, Fats: 17g, Total Carbs: 0.8g, Proteins: 32.7g

15. Thai Chicken Salad

Prep time: 20 minutes

Cook time: 0 minutes

Servings: 4

Ingredients

- 16 oz of shredded broccoli
- 1 cup of cooked and shredded chicken
- 1/2 cup of cucumber, diced
- 1/2 cup of sliced green onions
- 1/2 cup of salted peanuts
- 1/2 cup of diced red bell pepper
- 1/2 cup of peanut butter
- 3 tbsp of olive oil
- 3 tbsp of white vinegar
- 2 tbsp of soy sauce
- 1 tsp of sugar
- 1/2 tsp of minced garlic
- 1/2 tsp of crushed red pepper
- 1/2 tsp of black pepper
- 1 tsp of chopped cilantro

Instructions

Prepare the dressing by mixing all the ingredients except veggies and chicken in a bowl Cook veggies and chicken in the air fryer for about 7 minutes at 360°F. Sprinkle dressing over the salad and mix. Serve and enjoy!

Nutrition: Kcal: 237, Fats: 2g, Total Carbs: 20g, Proteins: 20g

16. Salmon And Sushi Bowl

Prep time: 15 minutes

Cook time: 5 minutes

Servings: 4

Ingredients

- 8 oz of smoked salmon
- 1 avocado
- 1 cucumber
- 3 oz of shredded carrots
- 1 tsp of toasted sesame seeds
- 1/2 sheet of nori
- 1 tsp of soy sauce and wasabi

For the Sushi Rice

- 24 oz. of riced cauliflower
- 1/2 cup of rice vinegar
- 3 finely chopped cloves garlic
- 2 tsp of grated ginger
- 1/2 tsp of sea salt

Instructions

Combine the rice vinegar, garlic, ginger, and salt in a mixing bowl. Sprinkle the vinegar mixture over riced cauliflower that has been prepared. Cook the veggies and salmon for about 7 minutes at 380°F. Serve with riced cauliflower.

Nutrition: Kcal: 237, Fats: 12g, Total Carbs: 10g, Proteins: 20g

17. Crispy Tilapia

Prep time: 15 minutes

Cook time: 5 minutes

Servings: 4

Ingredients

- 1 egg, whisked
- 4 fish fillets
- Olive oil spray
- 1 cup of breadcrumbs
- 1 1/2 tbsp of seafood seasoning

Instructions

Preheat the air fryer to 400°F. Dry fish fillets with a paper towel. Dip it in egg and then press the fillet into the mixture of breadcrumbs and seafood seasoning. Cook at 400°F for about 6 minutes. Serve and enjoy.

Nutrients: Kcal: 109, Fats: 2g, Total Carbs: 17g, Proteins: 5g

18. Teriyaki Glazed Salmon

Prep time: 15 minutes

Cook time: 5 minutes

Servings: 4

Ingredients

- 5 fillets of skinless salmon
- 1 cup of teriyaki sauce
- 3 tsp of salad dressing
- 5 cups of white rice
- 3 tsp of sesame seeds
- 2 sliced spring onions

Instructions

Preheat the air fryer for about 3 minutes at 200°F. In a shallow dish, place the salmon. Pour sauce over and flip to coat. Place salmon in a paper-lined basket. Cook for about 8 minutes. Cook the rice according to the package directions. Place the rice in a bowl. Add in the sesame seeds and mix well. Finish with the fish. Serve garnished with the leftover onion and sesame seeds.

Nutrients: Kcal: 506, Fats: 35g, Total Carbs: 10g, Proteins: 37g

19. Cauliflower with Buffalo Sauce

Prep time: 15 minutes

Cook time: 25 minutes

Servings: 4

Ingredients

- 1 cup of unsweetened almond milk
- 1 tbsp of apple cider vinegar
- 1/2 cauliflower
- 2 tsp of garlic powder
- 3/4 cup of all-purpose flour
- 2 tsp of smoked paprika
- 2 tsp of onion powder
- 5 tbsp of olive oil
- a third cup of buffalo sauce
- 1/4 cup of parsley
- 1 cup of celery stalks
- 1 cup of carrot sticks
- 1/2 cup of dairy-free coconut yogurt

Instructions

Preheat the air fryer for about 200°F. In a large mixing basin, combine almond milk and vinegar, then set aside for 5 minutes. Toss in the cauliflower to coat. In a separate large mixing bowl, combine the flour, paprika, garlic, and onion powder. Toss the cauliflower mixture until it is well covered. Lightly oil the air fryer basket. Place cauliflower mixture in a single layer in the basket and lightly coat with oil. Cook for 20 minutes. In a large mixing bowl, combine cauliflower and buffalo sauce. Sprinkle parsley over it and serve immediately with veggies and yogurt.

Nutrients: Kcal: 229, Fats: 12.8g, Total Carbs: 20.3g, Proteins: 6.2g

20. Coconut And Chicken Tenders

Prep time: 10 minutes

Cook time: 15 minutes

Servings: 2

Ingredients

- 1 egg
- 1 pound of chicken tenders
- 1/2 cup of pancake mix
- 1/4 of cup breadcrumbs
- 1 tsp of salt and pepper
- 1/4 cup of coconut flakes

Instructions

Combine the coconut flakes and breadcrumbs. Season the chicken with salt and pepper, then coat with breadcrumbs and coconut flakes. Air fry for 5 minutes per side at 390°F. Enjoy.

Nutrients: Kcal: 56, Fats: 4g, Total Carbs: 6g, Proteins: 2g

CHAPTER 4:

Snacks & Side Dishes

1. Buffalo Flavored Cauliflower

Prep time: 5 minutes

Cook time: 15 minutes

Servings: 4

Ingredients

- 1 small cut head of cauliflower
- Olive oil
- 1 cup of buffalo sauce
- 1 tbsp of butter melted
- salt and pepper for taste

Instructions

Spray the air fryer basket with olive oil. Mix everything in a bowl. Cook in the air fryer for almost 15 minutes at 400°F. Top with buffalo sauce and enjoy.

Nutrients: Kcal: 101, Fats: 7g, Total Carbs: 4g, Proteins: 6g

2. Cheesy Mushrooms

Prep time: 7 minutes

Cook time: 8 minutes

Servings: 4

Ingredients

- 6.5 oz of fresh mushrooms
- 3.5 oz of cream cheese, low-fat
- 0.5 cups of grated parmesan cheese, fat-free
- 0.5 cups of grated cheddar cheese, low-fat
- 1 tsp of Worcestershire sauce
- 1.5 minced cloves of garlic
- salt and pepper for taste

Instructions

Heat the cream cheese for 15 seconds to soften it. Mix everything in a medium bowl. Fill the mushrooms with the cheese mixture. Cook in the air fryer for about 8 minutes at 370°F. Serve and enjoy!

Nutrients: Kcal: 116, Fats: 8g, Total Carbs: 3g, Proteins: 8g

3. Stuffed Jalapenos

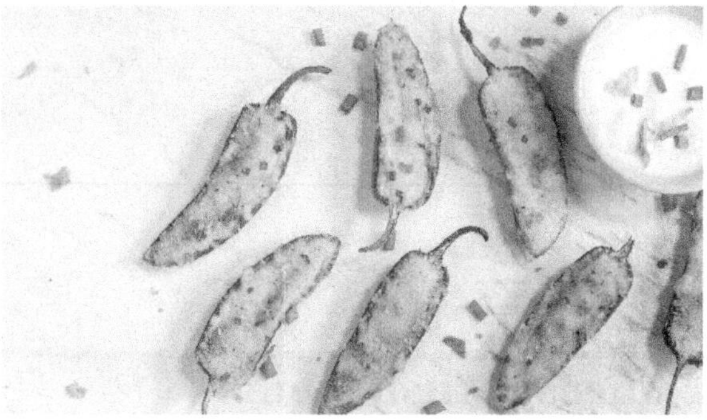

Prep time: 10 minutes

Cook time: 5 minutes

Servings: 4

Ingredients

- 8 of fresh jalapenos, halved
- 4.8 oz of low-fat cream cheese
- 1 cup of shredded cheddar cheese
- 1.6 slices of cooked bacon

Instruction:

Combine cream cheese and sour cream in a bowl. Heat for 15 seconds. Stir the cream cheese, crumbled bacon, and cheese in a mixing dish. Fill each jalapeño with the mixture. Cook in the air fryer for about 5 minutes at 370°F. Serve and enjoy.

Nutrients: Kcal: 62, Fats: 5g, Total Carbs: 3g, Proteins: 4g

4. Celeriac Fries

Prep time: 30 minutes

Cook time: 40 minutes

Servings: 4

Ingredients

- 1.5 celeriac root, sliced
- 4 tbsp of coconut oil
- 3 tsp of bagel seasoning

Instructions

Preheat the air fryer at 400°F. Soak celery slices in the water. Rinse and pat dry before tossing with coconut oil and spices. Cook for about 10 minutes in the air fryer. Serve with homemade mayo.

Nutrients: Kcal: 133, Fats:5g, Total Carbs: 11g, Proteins: 9g

5. Carrot Fries

Prep time: 15 minutes

Cook time: 20 minutes

Servings: 4

Ingredients

- 1 lb of carrots, sliced
- 1 tsp of garlic powder
- 1 tsp of paprika - 1 tsp of salt
- 1 tsp of onion powder
- 1 tsp of pepper - Low-fat cheese
- 1 tbsp of olive oil

For the Pesto Aioli

- 1 cup of mayonnaise - 1 tbsp of pesto
- 1 tbsp of squeezed lemon juice
- 1 tbsp of low-fat cheese

Instructions

Mix everything except pesto aioli items in a dish. Spray with olive oil and toss the carrots to cover in the spice and oil. Fry carrots in an air fryer for about 10 minutes at 400°F. Mix all the pesto aioli ingredients in a medium bowl. When the carrots are done, serve with the pesto aioli.

Nutrients: Kcal: 198, Fats: 3g, Total Carbs: 8g, Protein 5g

6. Rosemary & Sweet Potato Fries

Prep time: 15 minutes

Cook time: 15 minutes

Servings: 4

Ingredients

- Rosemary twigs
- 2 Sweet potatoes, sliced
- 2 tbsp of olive oil - 1/2 tsp of salt
- 1/2 tsp of Black pepper

Instructions

Mix everything in a bowl. Set aside for 5 minutes. Preheat the air fryer to 390°F. Fry the sweet potatoes for around 10 minutes. Serve and enjoy!

Nutrients: Kcal: 103, Fats: 5g, Total Carbs: 15g, Proteins: 10g

7. Green Beans With Bacon

Prep time: 5 minutes

Cook time: 15 minutes

Servings: 4

Ingredients

- 0.33 lb of green beans, cut
- 2 slices of bacon, sliced
- 1 tsp of black pepper
- 1 cup of halved cherry tomatoes

Instructions

Mix everything and add to the air fryer basket. Cook for 8 minutes at 370°F. Please rest for 7 minutes and then fry again for 7 minutes until golden brown. Serve and enjoy1

Nutrients: Kcal: 120, Fats: 10g, Total Carbs: 15g, Proteins: 15g

8. Crab Mushrooms

Prep time: 15 minutes

Cook time: 20 minutes

Servings: 4

Ingredients

- 1 lb of mushrooms
- 1 tsp of salt
- 1 diced red onion
- 1 oz of crab
- 1 cup of Breadcrumbs
- 1 egg
- 1 cup of low-fat cheese
- 1 tsp of oregano and hot sauce

Instructions

Preheat the air fryer at 400°F. Spray mushrooms with olive oil. Season them. Mix everything else in a bowl to make a mixture. Fill mushrooms with this mixture and garnish with cheese. Cook for about 9 minutes. Serve and enjoy.

Nutrients: Kcal: 33, Fats: 3g, Total Carbs: 1g, Proteins: 3g

9. Asparagus & Bacon

Prep time: 15 minutes

Cook time: 10 minutes

Servings: 4

Ingredients

- Cooking spray
- 10 slices of uncooked bacon
- 20 stalks of asparagus, sliced

Instructions

Spray the air fryer basket. Wrap asparagus stems with bacon slices. Cook at 390°F for 10 minutes. Season with freshly ground pepper. Serve and enjoy.

Nutrients: Kcal: 294, Total Carbs: 5g, Proteins: 10g, Fats: 8g

10. Gluten-Free Chickpeas

Prep time: 5 minutes

Cook time: 18 minutes

Servings: 4

Ingredients

- 15 oz can of chickpeas
- 1 tbsp of olive oil
- 2 tbsp of lemon juice
- 1 tsp of smoked paprika
- 1 tsp of ground cumin
- 1 tsp of granulated garlic and onion
- 1 tsp of salt and cayenne powder

Instructions

Preheat the air fryer at 390°F. Fry chickpeas in it. Mix all the other items in a bowl and pour on the chickpeas. Cook for about 5 minutes at 360°F. Serve and enjoy!

Nutrients: Kcal: 165, Fats: 15g, Total Carbs: 22g, Proteins: 25g

11. Low-Fat Cheesy Broccoli

Prep time: 10 minutes

Cook time: 15 minutes

Servings: 4

Ingredients

- 4 fresh broccoli florets
- 2 tbsp of olive oil
- 1 cup of low-fat cheese, grated
- 1 minced garlic clove
- 1/4 tsp of Italian seasoning
- 1/4 tsp of salt and pepper

Instructions

Mix everything in a bowl. Spray the air fryer basket. Cook for about 10 minutes at 370°F. Top with cheese.

Nutrients: Kcal: 131, Fats: 10g, Total Carbs: 7g, Proteins: 6g

12. Fried Eggplant

Prep time: 10 minutes

Cook time: 15 minutes

Servings: 4

Ingredients

- 1 large eggplant, diced
- 2 tbsp of olive oil
- 1 tsp of garlic powder
- 1 tsp of paprika
- 1 tsp of grated low-fat cheese

Instructions

Season the eggplant pieces. Set aside for 30 minutes. Mix everything in a dish. Cook for about 15 minutes at 370°F. Take out of the basket and serve!

Nutrients: Kcal: 126, Fats: 5g, Total Carbs: 7g, Proteins: 16g

13. Fried Biscuits

Prep time: 2 minutes

Cook time: 16 minutes

Servings: 4

Ingredients

- 8 buttermilk biscuits
- Cooking spray

Instructions

Preheat the air fryer at 320°F. Line the basket with baking parchment. Cook for about 16 minutes, turning midway along. Serve and enjoy.

Nutrients: Kcal: 212, Fats: 7g, Total Carbs: 10g, Protein 10g

14. Eggs With Bacon

Prep time: 10 minutes

Cook time: 15 minutes

Servings: 4

Ingredients

- 3 large eggs
- 1 cup of mayo
- 1 tsp of mustard
- 1 tsp of white vinegar
- 1 tsp of sugar
- 4 slices of cooked bacon
- 1 jalapeño pepper - salt and pepper

Instructions

Hard boil the egg and chop the veggies and the bacon into small pieces that could fit on top of the egg. After eggs are boiled, make sure to cut them in halves, and then spread the mayo and then the filling i=or topping. Serve ad enjoy

Nutrients: Kcal: 120, Fats: 10g, Total Carbs: 15g, Proteins: 20g

15. Low-Carb Mac & Cheese

Prep time: 15 minutes

Cook time: 60 minutes

Servings: 4

Ingredients

- 1 head cauliflower, cut
- A pinch of salt
- 3/4 cup of fat-free cream
- 2 tsp of garlic powder
- 3 cups of low-fat cheese
- 2 beaten eggs

Instructions

Preheat the air fryer at 400°F. Cook for about 15 minutes in the air fryer. Combine cream, salt, garlic powder, pepper, and eggs in a bowl. Spread the egg mixture over the cauliflower in the dish and mix. Cook for 40 minutes till the top is brown. Serve and enjoy.

Nutrients: Kcal: 567, Fats: 40g, Total Carbs: 11g, Proteins: 27g

16. Low-Carb Egg Salad

Prep time: 15 minutes

Cook time: 10 minutes

Servings: 4

Ingredients

- 3 eggs - 1 chopped cabbage
- 1 chopped cucumber
- 1 chopped carrot
- 1 chopped onion
- 1 chopped tomato
- 1/2 cup of shredded low-fat cheese

Instructions

Cook eggs in the air fryer for 15 minutes and prepare the mixture of greens. Mash eggs and transfer them to the greens mixture. Mix it thoroughly. Put the mixture again in the air fryer and top it with cheese. Cook for about 5 minutes and then serve.

Nutrients: Kcal: 150, Fats: 15g, Total Carbs: 10g, Proteins: 20g

17. Cauliflower Tots

Prep time: 15 minutes

Cook time: 20 minutes

Servings: 4

Ingredients

- 2 cups of cauliflower, diced
- 1 beaten egg
- 1 cup of low-carb breadcrumbs
- 1 cup of low-fat cheese

Instructions

Cook cauliflower in the air fryer for 10 minutes. Mix other ingredients in a bowl. Toss cauliflower pieces in it. Top them with cheese and cook in the air fryer for about 5 more minutes. Serve with your favorite sauce and enjoy.

Nutrients: Kcal: 136, Fats: 9g, Total carbs: 6g, Proteins: 10g

18. Fried Pickles

Prep time: 10 minutes

Cook time: 10 minutes

Servings: 4

Ingredients

- 4 cups of pickle slices
- 2 tbsp of coconut flour
- 2 large eggs
- 2 cups of pork rinds
- 1 tsp of garlic powder
- 1 tsp of paprika
- 1 tsp of black pepper
- Salt for taste

Instructions

Preheat the air fryer at 400°F. Stir the pickles gently with the coconut flour to cover both sides. Whisk the egg in another bowl. Combine all the other ingredients in a separate bowl. Dip pickles in egg wash and then in pork rind mixture. Cook in the air fryer for about 10 minutes. Serve with your favorite ranch, and enjoy!

Nutrients: Kcal: 113, Fats: 7g, Total Carbs: 7g, Proteins: 13g

19. Tilapia Fish Sticks

Prep time: 10 minutes

Cook time: 15 minutes

Servings: 4

Ingredients

- 12 oz of tilapia loins, cut
- 4 tbsp of mayo
- 1 tsp of garlic powder
- 1 tsp of paprika
- 3.25 oz of pork rinds
- 1/2 cup of low-fat cheese

Instructions

Mix rinds, spices, and breadcrumbs in a dish. Fill a ziplock bag with mayo. Pour it on fish pieces and then roll them into the crumb mixture. Cook in the air fryer at 380°F for 15 minutes. Serve and enjoy.

Nutrients: Kcal: 75, Fats: 10g, Total Carbs: 1g, Proteins: 20g

CHAPTER 5:

Vegetarian Recipes

1. Zucchini Skins

Prep time: 10 minutes

Cook time: 13 minutes

Servings: 4

Ingredients

- 2 medium-sized zucchinis, diced
- 2 tbsp of olive oil
- 1 tsp of garlic powder
- 1 tsp of onion powder
- 1 tsp of salt
- 1 tsp of black pepper
- 1 cup of sour cream
- 2 tbsp of chopped chives
- 3 oz of shredded fat-free cheese

Instructions

Combine the garlic, onion powder, salt, and pepper in a small bowl. Brush the zucchini slices lightly with oil and season them. Cook in the air fryer for about 8 minutes at 400°F. Top with cheese. Cook for 5 more minutes. Serve with sour cream and enjoy.

Nutrients: Kcal: 197, Fats: 15g, Total Carbs: 4g, Proteins: 7g

2. Lupini Beans

Prep time: 5 minutes

Cook time: 18 minutes

Servings: 4

Ingredients

- 20 oz of Lupini beans
- 1 lime juice
- 1 tsp of olive oil
- 1 tsp of chili powder
- Pepper and salt, as per taste

Instructions

In a medium mixing bowl, combine all the ingredients. Cook in the air fryer at 380°F for 10 minutes. Serve and enjoy it as a snack.

Nutrients: Kcal: 197, Fats: 10g, Total Carbs: 4g, Proteins: 15g

3. Zucchini Chips

Prep time: 10 minutes

Cook time: 10 minutes

Servings: 4

Ingredients

- 2 Zucchinis, sliced
- 2 tbsp of Olive oil
- Pinch of sea salt and black pepper

Instructions

Preheat the air fryer at 320°F. In a large bowl, mix all the ingredients. Spray the air fryer basket with oil. Cook zucchini for about about 10 minutes. Serve and enjoy.

Nutrients: Kcal: 39, Fats: 2g, Total Carbs: 2g, Proteins: 3g

4. Stuffed Baby Artichokes

Prep time: 10 minutes

Cook time: 15 minutes

Servings: 4

Ingredients

- 20 of the baby artichokes, cut
- 1 1/2 cups of water
- 1/2 cup of lemon juice
- 1/2 tbsp of olive oil
- 1/2 tsp of salt and black pepper
- 1 cup of cream cheese, fat-free
- 1 cup of frozen spinach
- 3 cloves of minced garlic
- 1/2 cup of grated low-fat cheese

Instructions

Soak artichokes in lemon water. Mix spinach, garlic, and cheese in a bowl. Remove the artichokes from the water and pat dry. Add spices and olive oil to them. Cook for 10 minutes at 400°F in the air fryer. Serve and enjoy.

Nutrients: Kcal: 175, Fats: 12g, Total carbs: 13g, Proteins: 10g

5. Low-Fat Cheese Sticks

Prep time: 10 minutes

Cook time: 10 minutes

Servings: 4

Ingredients

- 8 mozzarella sticks
- 1/2 cup of almond flour
- 1/2 cup of finely grated low-fat cheese
- 1 egg
- 1 tsp of garlic powder
- 1 tsp of oregano
- 1/2 tsp of salt and black pepper

Instructions

Beat the egg. Mix all the ingredients except for the mozzarella sticks in a separate bowl. Now dip the sticks in the egg and then into the dry mixture. Meanwhile, spray the air fryer basket with oil, add the sticks, and cook for 10 minutes at 380°F. Serve and enjoy!

Nutrients: Kcal: 72, Fats: 5g, Total carbs: 1g, Proteins: 5g

6. Pumpkin Fries

Prep time: 10 minutes

Cook time: 15 minutes

Servings: 4

Ingredients

- 1 pumpkin, cut
- 1 tbsp of olive oil
- 2 tbsp of chili lime seasoning

Instructions

Combine the olive oil, fries, and spices in a mixing bowl. Cook in the air fryer for 12 minutes at 400°F. Serve with your favorite dip, and enjoy.

Nutrients: Kcal: 43, Fats: 7g, Total Carbs: 3g, Proteins: 2g

7. Jicama Fries

Prep time: 15 minutes

Cook time: 30 minutes

Servings: 4

Ingredients

- 1 jicama, cut
- 1 tsp of salt
- 2 tbsp of olive oil
- 2 tap of garlic powder
- 1 tsp of oregano, dried
- 1 tsp of onion powder
- 1 tsp of black pepper
- 2 tsp of paprika
- 1 tsp of cayenne pepper
- 1 tsp of thyme, dried
- 1 tsp of basil dried

Instructions

Combine the herbs and spices in a mixing bowl. Season the fries. Spray the jicama sticks gently with oil. Cook in the air fryer for 15 minutes at 400°F. Serve and enjoy!

Nutrients: Kcal: 137, Fats: 7g, Total Carbs: 10g, Proteins: 10g

8. Mushroom Fries

Prep time: 19 minutes

Cook time: 10 minutes

Servings: 4

Ingredients

- 2 portobello mushrooms, cut
- 1/2 tsp of black pepper
- 2 beaten eggs
- 1/2 tsp of garlic powder
- 1 cup of almond flour
- 1/2 tsp of salt
- 1/2 tsp of onion powder

Instructions

Mix everything in a bowl. Then spray a little oil in the air fryer basket and toss the fries in it. Cook for about 15 minutes at 400°F. Serve with your favorite dip, and enjoy!

Nutrients: Kcal: 200, Fats: 5g, Total Carbs: 2g, Proteins: 10g

9. Fried Reddish

Prep time: 10 minutes

Cook time: 15 minutes

Servings: 4

Ingredients

- 12 oz of radishes, halved
- Parsley flakes
- 2 tsp of olive oil
- 1 crushed clove of garlic
- Pinch of salt
- 4 tbsp of grated low-fat cheese
- 1 tsp of red pepper

Instructions

Cook radish in the air fryer for about 8 minutes at 400°F. In a bowl, combine all the other ingredients. Toss cooked radishes in it and fry again for about 3 minutes.

Nutrients: Kcal: 115, Fats: 7g, Total Carbs: 5g, Proteins: 5g

10. Cheesy Eggplant

Prep time: 10 minutes

Cook time: 20 minutes

Servings: 4

Ingredients

- 1 medium-sized eggplant
- 2 cups of breadcrumbs
- 1 tbsp of garlic powder
- 1 tbsp of dried parsley
- 1/2 tsp of salt
- 1/4 tsp of black pepper
- 2 eggs - 1 cup of tomato sauce
- 1 cup of shredded low-fat cheese
- Freshly chopped basil

Instructions

Make a breadcrumb mixture with the ingredients mentioned above. Preheat the air fryer at 390°F. Toss eggplant slices in the dry mixture. Spray the air fryer basket. Cook for about 8 minutes. Garnish with the basil and enjoy!

Nutrients: Kcal: 178, Fats: 5g, Total Carbs: 5g, Proteins: 7g

11. Cauliflower Gnocchi

Prep time: 10 minutes

Cook time: 15 minutes

Servings: 4

Ingredients

- 1 cauliflower head, cut
- 1/2 cup of lupin flour
- 1/2 cup of oat fiber
- 1 tsp of salt

Instructions

Boil the cauliflower till soft, and then mash them. Mix them with the other ingredients until you get the dough consistency and make them oval-shaped. Preheat the air fryer and spray the basket with olive oil. Toss the dough and cook for 10 minutes at 350°F until golden brown.

Nutrients: Kcal: 115, Fats: 1g, Total Carbs: 10g, Proteins: 9g

12. Lupini Bean Falafel

Prep time: 10 minutes

Cook time: 20 minutes

Servings: 4

Ingredients

- 2 cups of lupini beans
- 1 chopped onion
- 3 chopped cloves of garlic
- 1 tbsp of tahini
- 2 tsp of cumin
- 3 tsp of coriander powder
- 3 tbsp of parsley, fresh
- 2 tbsp of fresh cilantro
- 1/2 tsp of baking soda
- 2 tbsp of lupin flour
- 1/2 tsp of salt and black pepper

Instructions

Place all the ingredients except the lupin flour in the processor and mix until smooth. Now mix it with the flour and make circular pieces. Preheat the air fryer, place the falafel coated with olive oil spray and cook for about 20 minutes at 350°F. Serve and enjoy.

Nutrients: Kcal: 24, Fats: 1g, Total Carbs: 4g, Proteins: 5g

13. Crispy Tofu

Prep time: 12 minutes

Cook time: 15 minutes

Servings: 4

Ingredients

- 16 oz of tofu, diced
- 2 tsp of tamari
- 2 minced cloves of garlic
- 2 tsp of grated ginger
- 1/2 tsp of red chili flakes
- 2 tbsp of avocado oil

Instructions

Marinade the tofu by mixing all the ingredients and let it be for 15 minutes. Air fry the tofu for about 15 minutes at 350°F. Serve and enjoy.

Nutrients: Kcal: 144, Fats: 15g, Total Carbs: 4g, Proteins: 16g

14. Zucchini Fritters

Prep time: 10 minutes

Cook time: 15 minutes

Servings: 4

Ingredients

- 1 medium-sized zucchini, cut
- 1 tsp of sea salt
- 1 large egg
- 1 cup of almond flour
- 1 cup of grated low-fat cheese
- 1 tsp of baking powder
- 1 tsp of lemon pepper
- 1 tsp of garlic powder

- 1 tsp of smoked paprika
- 1 tsp of Italian seasoning
- 1 finely sliced green onions
- olive oil spray

Instructions

Grate the zucchini's and drain excess water. Make the patties by mixing all the above ingredients. Cook them at 200°F for 20 minutes. Serve and enjoy!

Nutrients: Kcal: 68, Fats: 5g, Total Carbs: 3g, Proteins: 5g

15. Avocado Tacos

Prep time: 15 minutes

Cook time: 5 minutes

Servings: 4

Ingredients

- 4 avocados, sliced
- 3 tsp of taco seasoning
- 1 1/2 cups of breadcrumbs
- Corn tortillas

Toppings

- Tomato
- Cilantro
- Shredded cabbage
- Corn
- Lime wedges

Instructions

Coat avocado slices with all the ingredients except for the topping ingredients. Cook for 4 minutes at 375°F. Warm the tortillas. Now make tacos by stuffing the tacos with fried avocados and toppings. Serve and enjoy!

Nutrients: Kcal: 500, Fats: 20g, Total Carbs: 30g, Proteins: 20g

16. General Tso's Cauliflower

Prep time: 10 minutes

Cook time: 20 minutes

Servings: 4

Ingredients

- 2 oz of cauliflower florets, cut
- 1 egg
- 1 cup of panko breadcrumbs

For the Sauce

- 3 tsp of brown sugar
- 1 cup of hoisin sauce
- 1 cup of ketchup
- 2 cloves of garlic
- 1 tsp of minced ginger
- 1 cup of low sodium soy sauce
- 1 cup of rice vinegar
- 1 tsp of sriracha
- 1 tsp of corn starch mixed with water
- Sesame seeds and scallions for topping

Instructions

Coat the small floret cauliflowers with the egg mixture, then mix with bread crumbs. Cook them in the air fryer for 20 minutes until crispy brown at 250°F. Meanwhile, prepare the sauce ingredients. Serve fried cauliflowers with sauce.

Nutrients: Kcal: 131, Fats: 4g, Total Carbs: 12g, Proteins: 4g

17. Mushroom Bites

Prep time: 20 minutes

Cook time: 7 minutes

Servings: 4

Ingredients

- 4 large mushrooms, diced
- 1 tbsp of unsalted butter
- 1 minced clove of garlic
- 1 cup of onion, minced
- 1 oz of cream cheese, low-fat

- 1 tsp of thyme leaves
- 1 tsp of Worcestershire sauce
- 1 tsp of chopped parsley
- 1 cup of low-fat cheese - 1 tsp of pepper

Instructions

Make the filling for the mushrooms and fill them. Now cook them in an air fryer for about 10 minutes at 350°F. Serve and enjoy!

Nutrients: Kcal: 250, Fats: 12g, Total Carbs: 20g, Proteins: 15g

18. Stuffed Olives

Prep time: 10 minutes

Cook time: 20 minutes

Servings: 4

Ingredients

- 2 cups of cheese stuffed olives
- 1/2 cup of gluten-free flour
- 1 cup of panko breadcrumbs
- 1/2 tsp of garlic powder
- A pinch of oregano
- 2 eggs

Instructions

Combine the flour, oregano, and garlic powder in a mixing basin. In a separate dish, mix the eggs. Add the breadcrumbs to a third bowl. Dip each olive in the flour mixture, then in the egg, and last in the breadcrumbs. Repeat with the remaining olives and set them in a lightly sprayed air fry basket. Cook for 5 minutes at 500°F. Serve and enjoy.

Nutrients: Kcal: 200, Fats: 10g, Total Carbs: 10g, Proteins: 10g

19. Avocado Rolls

Prep time: 10 minutes

Cook time: 15 minutes

Servings: 4

Ingredients

- 1 avocado, diced
- 3 chopped onions
- 2 tomatoes, chopped
- 1 tbsp of lime juice
- 1/4 tsp of garlic powder
- 1/2 tsp of cayenne pepper
- 1/2 tsp of salt
- 1/2 tsp of black pepper

Instructions

Mix all the ingredients. Make rolls. Cook in the air fryer at 400°F for about 10 minutes and serve.

Nutrients: Kcal: 200, Fats: 11g, Total Carbs: 10g, Proteins: 5g

20. Sweet Carrots Dish

Prep time: 10 minutes

Cook time: 10 minutes

Servings: 4

Ingredients

- 2 cups of carrots
- Salt & black pepper
- 1 tbsp of brown sugar
- 1/2 tbsp of melted butter, unsalted

Instructions

Mix everything in a dish. Cook in the air fryer for around 10 minutes at 350°F. Serve and enjoy.

Nutrients: Kcal 100, Fats: 2g, Total Carbs: 7g, Proteins: 4g

21. Summer Squash

Prep time: 10 minutes

Cook time: 10 minutes

Servings: 4

Ingredients

- 4 cups of sliced squash
- 3 tbsp of olive oil
- 1/2 tsp of salt
- 1/2 tsp of pepper
- 1/8 tsp of cayenne pepper
- 3/4 cup of breadcrumbs
- 3/4 cup of low-fat cheese, grated

Instructions

Mix seasonings and oil with squash in a bowl. Mix cheese and crumbs in another bowl. Dip squash in crumbs and place in basket in a single layer. Cook in the air fryer for around 10 minutes at 350°F. Serve and enjoy.

Nutrients: Kcal 203, Fats: 14g, Total Carbs: 13g, Proteins: 6g

22. Collard Greens

Prep time: 10 minutes

Cook time: 10 minutes

Servings: 4

Ingredients

- 1 bunch of collard greens, trimmed
- 2 tbsp of olive oil
- 2 tbsp of tomato puree
- 1 chopped yellow onion
- 3 minced garlic cloves
- Salt & black pepper, as per taste
- 1 tbsp of balsamic vinegar
- 1 tsp of brown sugar

Instructions

Mix everything in a bowl. Cook in the air fryer for about 10 minutes at 320°F. Serve and enjoy.

Nutrients: Kcal 121, Fats: 3g, Total Carbs: 7g, Proteins: 3g

23. Garlic & Rosemary Sprouts

Prep time: 10 minutes

Cook time: 15 minutes

Servings: 4

Ingredients

- 3 tbsp of olive oil
- 2 minced garlic cloves
- 1/2 tsp of salt
- 1/4 tsp of pepper
- 1 pound of Brussels sprouts, halved
- 1/2 cup of breadcrumbs
- 1 1/2 tsp of rosemary, minced

Instructions

Microwave the first four ingredients in a bowl for around 30 seconds. Top sprouts with the mixture. Cook for about 12 minutes in the fryer at 350°F. Mix crumbs with the rest of the oil mixture and rosemary. Sprinkle this on sprouts and enjoy.

Nutrients: Kcal 164, Fats: 11g, Total Carbs: 15g, Proteins: 5g

CHAPTER 6:

Fish & Seafood

1. Fish & Chips

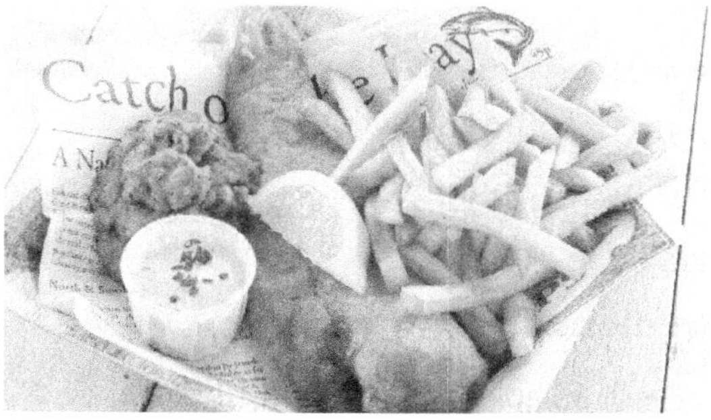

Prep time: 10 minutes

Cook time: 30 minutes

Servings: 4

Ingredients

- 6 oz of cod fillets - 1 1/2 cups of almond flour - 2 eggs - 1/2 tsp of sea salt
- 1 1/2 tsp of Old Bay seasoning
- 1 tsp of dried parsley
- 1/2 tsp of garlic powder
- 1/2 tsp of black pepper

Instructions

Preheat the air fryer for 10 minutes at 390°F. Whisk egg in one bowl and mix all other items except cod in another bowl. Dip cod fillet in egg mixture and then in dry mixture. Spray the air fryer basket and cook fillets for about 20 minutes. Serve with fries and sauce.

Nutrients: Kcal: 430, Fats: 15g, Total Carbs: 14g, Proteins: 35g

2. Cheesy White Fish

Prep time: 10 minutes

Cook time: 15 minutes - Servings: 4

Ingredients

- 2 tilapia fillets
- 1 tbsp of olive oil
- 1/2 cup of grated low-fat cheese
- Salt and black pepper, for taste
- 1/2 tsp of garlic powder
- 1/2 tsp of onion powder
- 1/2 tsp of smoked paprika
- Finely chopped parsley
- lemon wedge

Instructions

Preheat the air fryer at 380°F for 5 minutes. Season fish with all the ingredients except cheese. Then cover it with cheese. Spray the air fryer basket with oil. Cook for about 20 minutes. Garnish with parsley or lemon wedges and serve.

Nutrients: Kcal: 338, Fats: 17g, Total Carbs: 2g, Proteins: 44g

3. Breaded Cod

Prep time: 10 minutes

Cook time: 15 minutes

Servings: 4

Ingredients

- 10 boneless and skinless cod
- 2 cups of pork dust
- 1 cup of coconut flour
- 2 Eggs
- 1 cup of almond milk
- Salt and pepper for taste
- Coconut oil spray

Instructions

Preheat the air fryer at 400°F. Add coconut flour in one bowl. Mix eggs and almond milk in another bowl. Add pork dust in a separate bowl. Coat cod with each mixture one by one. Then cook for about 15 minutes and serve with sauce.

Nutrients: Kcal: 330, Fats: 20g, Total Carbs: 20g, Proteins: 35g

4. Spanish Cod

Prep time: 5 minutes

Cook time: 15 minutes

Servings: 4

Ingredients

- 1 pack of frozen cod fillets
- 2 tins of chopped tomatoes
- 1 cup of white rice
- 2 cloves of garlic
- Fresh parsley
- 1 lemon

Instructions

Preheat the air fryer at 300°F for 10 minutes. Add the tomatoes and the cod fillet in the basket with olive oil and cook for about 15 minutes. Meanwhile, boil the rice. Serve and enjoy!

Nutrients: Kcal: 455, Fats: 8g, Total Carbs: 40g, Proteins: 30g

5. Shrimp Caprese Bites

Prep time: 10 minutes

Cook time: 15 minutes

Servings: 4

Ingredients

- 12 cocktail shrimp
- 1 tsp of lemon juice
- 1 tbs of olive oil
- 1 1/3 oz of low-fat cheese
- 2 halved cherry tomatoes
- 12 basil leaves
- Salt and pepper to taste

Instructions

Preheat the air fryer for about 10 minutes at 300°F. Toss the shrimps in the lemon, basil, salt and pepper mixture. Take a toothpick and insert shrimp, cheese cube and tomatoes. Now cook for 15 minutes with occasional flipping. Serve with your favorite sauce and enjoy!

Nutrients: Kcal: 300, Fats: 20g, Total Carbs: 30g, Proteins: 30g

6.Tuna Tartare

Prep time: 5 minutes

Cook time: 3 minutes

Servings: 4

Ingredients

- 2 inches of Lotus roots, sliced
- 1/4 cup of olive oil
- 1/2 lb of Sushi tuna
- 1 stalk of green onion
- 4 shiso leaves
- 2 tsp of soy sauce
- 1/8 tsp of salt
- 1 tsp of sesame oil
- 1/8 tsp of sesame seeds

Instructions

Air fry lotus roots in the air fryer at 300°F for 15 minutes. Then mince the tuna and mix with all the other Ingredients. Place the mixture on the fried lotus roots. Serve and enjoy!

Nutrients: Kcal: 74, Fats: 6g, Total Carbs: 1g, Proteins: 5g

7. Honey Walnut Shrimps

Prep time: 10 minutes

Cook time: 5 minutes

Servings: 4

Ingredients

- 1 lb of peeled shrimps
- 1/2 cup of almond flour
- 2 tbsp of low-fat cheese
- 2 eggs
- 1/3 cup of water
- Olive oil
- 1 stalk of green onions, diced
- 1/2 cup of caramelized walnuts

Instructions

Prepare the batter for coating the shrimps by mixing all the ingredients. After that, add them to the preheated air fryer at 400°F for 15 minutes with occasional flipping. Serve and enjoy.

Nutrients: Kcal: 252, Fats: 60g, Total Carbs: 10g, Proteins: 30g

8. Tuna Tacos

Prep time: 10 minutes

Cook time: 10 minutes

Servings: 4

Ingredients

- 4 oz of fresh tuna steaks
- 2 tsp of Mexican seasoning
- 6 low-carb tortillas
- 1.5 cups of shredded red cabbage
- 6 sliced radishes
- 1 diced avocado
- 6 tbsp of spicy mayo

Instructions

Pat the tuna dry and then cook in the air fryer for about 15 minutes and add seasoning in it. Assemble the rest of the filling for tacos and add in tortilla wraps one by one. Serve and enjoy!

Nutrients: Kcal: 280, Fats: 19g, Total Carbs: 25g, Protein: 20g

9. Healthy Salmon

Prep time: 15 minutes

Cook time: 15 minutes

Servings: 4

Ingredients

- 6 oz of Salmon fillets
- 3 tbsp soy sauce
- 3 tbsp of brown sugar
- 2 tsp toasted sesame oil
- 2 tsp of ginger garlic paste
- 2 tsp of rice vinegar

Instructions

Marinade the salmon with the mixture of the above Ingredients and set it aside for 1 hour. Then take it out and cook in the air fryer for 30 minutes at 300°F. Garnish it with scallions and sesame seeds. Serve with vegetables and enjoy!

Nutrients: Kcal: 192, Fats: 7g, Total Carbs: 2g, Proteins: 30g

10. Prawn Stir Fry

Prep time: 10 minutes

Cook time: 18 minutes

Servings: 4

Ingredients

- 1 tsp of olive oil
- 4 sliced red chilies
- 1 sliced clove garlic
- 1 lb of Prawns
- 1/2 tsp of red pepper
- 1/2 head of broccoli, diced
- 1 tbsp of soy sauce
- 1/2 cup of lime juice - 1/2 of courgette
- Coriander and onion, sliced

Instructions

Preheat the air fryer at 300°F for 15 minutes. Mix prawns, salt, oil, garlic and chili in a bowl. Cook for 3 minutes with occasional flipping and stirring. Saute veggies in a pan. Mix prawn and veggies in a dish. Add soy sauce and lime juice. Serve and enjoy!

Nutrients: Kcal: 300, Fats: 7g, Total Carbs: 17g, Proteins: 33g

11. Prawn Noodles

Prep time: 15 minutes

Cook time: 20 minutes

Servings: 4

Ingredients

- 1 lb of deveined prawns
- 2 packets of shirataki noodles
- 1 Thai chili pepper
- 2 minced cloves of garlic

- 1 tbsp of minced ginger
- 1 bunch of cilantros
- 2 sliced spring onions
- 1 deseeded green pepper
- 1/2 of deseeded red pepper
- 1 1/2 chopped oyster mushrooms
- 2 cups of bean sprouts
- 4 tbsp of fish sauce
- 2 tbsp of fresh lime juice
- 1 tsp of olive oil - 1/2 tsp sea salt

Instructions

Boil the noodles. Preheat the air fryer at 300°F for 15 minutes. Mix everything except veggies and mushrooms in a bowl. Cook for about 10 minutes. Saute veggies and mushrooms for 15 minutes in a pan. Add in all the prepared mixtures and mix thoroughly, now add fish sauce and mix well. Garnish with greens. Serve and enjoy!

Nutrients: Kcal: 390, Fats: 20g, Total Carbs: 8g, Proteins: 25g

12. Stir Fried Shrimps

Prep time: 10 minutes

Cook time: 20 minutes

Servings: 4

Ingredients

- 4 tbsp of olive oil - 1 lb of shrimps
- 8 cups of vegetables, diced

Instructions

Saute veggies in a pan. Preheat the air fry for 15 minutes at 300°F. Spray oil on shrimps. Cook in the air fryer for 20 minutes. Now add them to a large bowl and mix with the prepared vegetables and sauce. Serve and enjoy.

Nutrients: Kcal: 204, Fats: 13g, Total Carbs: 10g, Proteins: 17g

13. Fish & Veggies

Prep time: 20 minutes

Cook time: 5 minutes

Servings: 4

Ingredients

- 4 fish fillets, chopped
- 3 sliced bell peppers
- 2 zucchini courgettes
- 1 tbsp of fish seasoning
- 2 tbsp of olive oil - 1 tsp of salt

Instructions

Make vegetable noodles. Add salt to it and set aside for 10 minutes. Then drain them. Season the fish and cook in the air fryer for about 20 minutes. Sauté the peppers in a saucepan. Now mix everything in a bowl and serve on a platter.

Nutrients: Kcal: 107, Fats: 8g, Total Carbs: 9g, Proteins: 5g

14. Salmon & Veggies

Prep time: 15 minutes

Cook time: 20 minutes

Servings: 4

Ingredients

- 4 salmon filets
- 3 cups of sliced mushrooms
- 1 bunch of asparagus, chopped
- 2 heads of broccoli. cut
- 1 lemon - 1/2 cup of maple syrup
- 2 tbsp of avocado
- 1 tbsp of brown sugar
- 1 tsp of garlic powder
- 2 tsp of black pepper and salt

Instructions

Combine all the Ingredients except salmon in a bowl. Prepare the sauce and coat the salmon evenly. Now add the salmon with veggies. Cook for 20 minutes at 400°F. Serve and enjoy!

Nutrients: Kcal: 300, Fats: 20g, Total Carbs: 20g, Protein: 35g

15. Healthy White Fish Sticks

Prep time: 10 minutes

Cook time: 10 minutes

Servings: 4

Ingredients

- 1 tsp of paprika
- 1/2 tsp of salt
- 2 tbsp of water
- Olive oil spray
- 1/4 cup of mayo
- 1/2 tsp of dried dill
- 1 tsp of garlic powder
- 1/2 cup of almond flour
- 2 tbsp of yellow mustard
- 1/2 tsp of black pepper
- 1/2 cup of crushed pork rinds

- 1 lb of white fish, cut into sticks

Instructions

Preheat the air fryer at 350°F for 15 minutes. Mix all the Ingredients except the fish in a dish. Coat the fish from all sides evenly. Now cook in the air fryer for 20 minutes. Serve and enjoy!

Nutrients: Kcal: 236, Fats: 15g, Total Carbs: 2g, Proteins: 25g

16. Salmon Cakes

Prep time: 15 minutes

Cook time: 10 minutes

Servings: 4

Ingredients

- 1 can of salmon
- 1 beaten egg
- 1 cup of panko
- 4 tbsp of mayo
- 1 tbsp of olive oil
- 1 diced celery stalk
- 1/2 tsp of onion powder
- 1/2 tsp of black pepper
- 1/2 tsp of garlic powder
- 2 tbsp of chopped parsley
- 1/2 tsp of old bay seasoning
- 1/2 tsp of smoked paprika
- 1 tsp of Worcestershire sauce

Instructions

Mix everything and make small patties. Preheat the air fryer at 350°F for 5 minutes. Now put the patties in the air fryer and cook for 15 minutes. Serve and enjoy!

Nutrients: Kcal: 208, Fats: 25g, Total Carbs: 20g, Proteins: 18g

17. Lobster Tail

Prep time: 10 minutes

Cook time: 20 minutes

Servings: 4

Ingredients

- 6 oz of lobster tails
- 1 tbsp of minced garlic
- 1 tsp of salt
- 1 tsp of chopped chives
- 1 tsp of lemon juice
- 2 tbsp of unsalted butter, melted

Instructions

Prepare the batter mixture by combing butter, garlic, salt, lemon juice and chives. Cut the lobsters in a butterfly shape. Preheat the air fryer at 350°F. Place the lobster with the top covered with the batter. Cook for 10 minutes and then serve!

Nutrients: Kcal: 109, Fats: 10g, Total Carbs: 2g, Proteins: 12g

18. Catfish With Tartar Sauce

Prep time: 5 minutes

Cook time: 20 minutes

Servings: 4

Ingredients

- 2/4 cups of cornmeal
- 3 tsp of Cajun seasoning
- 4 catfish fillets

For the Tartar Sauce

- 1/4 cup of dill pickles
- 1/2 cup of mayo
- 1 tbsp of lemon juice
- 1 tsp of Cajun seasoning

Instructions

Make the mixture of corneal and spices. Coat the fish with it. Cook in preheated air fryer for about 10 minutes. Prepare the tartar sauce and serve!

Nutrients: Kcal: 481, Fats: 24g, Total Carbs: 19g, Proteins: 30g

19. Tasty Scallops

Prep time: 5 minutes

Cook time: 5 minutes

Servings: 4

Ingredients

- 8 scallops
- olive oil
- sea salt
- pepper

Instructions

Preheat the air fryer. Mix everything in a bowl. Cook for 5 minutes at 300°F. Serve and enjoy!

Nutrients: Kcal: 200, Fats: 20g, Total Carbs: 20g, Proteins: 30g

20. Siracha & Honey Cod

Prep time: 10 minutes

Cook time: 15 minutes

Servings: 4

Ingredients

- 3/4 cups of panko
- 2 tbsp of Sriracha
- 2 tbsp of honey
- 2 skinless cod fillets
- Cooking spray

Instructions

Mix all the Ingredients and then add in the preheated air fryer. Cook for 15 minutes at 350°F and serve.

Nutrients: Kcal: 200, Fats: 15g, Total Carbs: 20g, Proteins: 15g

CHAPTER 7:

Chicken & Poultry Recipes

1. Healthy Asian Chicken

Prep time: 30 minutes

Cook time: 15 minutes

Servings: 2

Ingredients

- 1 egg
- Breadcrumbs
- 1/4 tsp of pepper
- 1/4 cup of water
- 1 tbsp of soy sauce
- 1/4 tsp of chili pepper
- 1 clove of garlic, minced
- 1/4 tsp of five-spice
- 2 green onions, minced
- 1 lb of boneless chicken
- 1/2 tsp of potato starch

Instructions

In a large mixing basin, combine all ingredients except the egg, starch, and water. Combine the ingredients and add diced chicken to the bowl. Prepare the chicken by coating it with the mixture and setting it aside for 30 minutes. Whisk together water and egg in a separate dish, then stir in starch. Cook the chicken in the air fryer at 350°F for about 15 minutes after coating it with the sauce. Season it with pepper and salt before serving.

Nutrients: Kcal: 310, Fats: 16g, Total Carbs: 21g, Proteins: 32g

2. Sweet Lime Chicken

Prep time: 6 hours

Cook time: 20 minutes

Servings: 4

Ingredients

- 1/2 tsp of sea salt
- 14 chicken wings
- 2 tbsp of honey
- 2 tbsp of lime juice
- 2 tbsp of soya sauce
- 1/2 crushed black pepper
- 1/4 tsp of pepper powder, white

Instructions

In a large mixing bowl, combine all ingredients and coat the wings with it. Refrigerate for about 6 hours after covering with plastic wrap. Place the wings in the air fryer basket and cook for about 7 minutes at 350°F. Cook for another 7 minutes on the other side. Cook for another 4 minutes after flipping. Serve and enjoy.

Nutrients: Kcal 310, Fats: 19g, Total Carbs: 22g, Proteins: 39g

3. Low Carb Healthy Chicken

Prep time: 10 minutes

Cook time: 20 minutes

Servings: 6

Ingredients

- 2 eggs
- 1 cup of Pork rinds
- 1/4 tsp of dried thyme
- 1/2 tsp of sea salt
- 1/2 tsp of garlic powder
- 1/4 cup of coconut flour
- 1/4 tsp of black pepper
- 2 1/2 lbs of chicken drumsticks
- 1 tsp of smoked paprika

Instructions

Combine the coconut flour, black pepper, and sea salt in a mixing bowl. Set it aside. In a separate dish, whisk the eggs. In another small bowl, combine all the spices. Dredge the chicken in the flour mixture before dipping it in the eggs. Then coat with spices and cook for about 20 minutes at 400°F in an air fryer. Serve and enjoy.

Nutrients: Kcal 273, Fats: 15g, Total Carbs: 2g, Proteins: 28g

4. Mushrooms With Chicken Noodles

Prep time: 30 minutes

Cook time: 17 minutes

Servings: 4

Ingredients

- 1 sliced onion
- 6 tsp of sesame oil
- 1 tsp of sambal
- 1/4 cup of soy sauce
- 3 tsp of sesame seeds
- 2 cloves of garlic
- 7 ounces of glasswort
- 12 ounces of thigh chicken fillets, diced
- 2/3 cup of shiitake mushrooms
- 12 ounces of wheat noodles, boiled
- 2/3 cup of chestnut mushrooms
- 5 ounces of bean sprouts

Instructions

Combine the chopped garlic, sambal, and soy sauce in a large mixing bowl. Soak the chicken in this mixture for about 30 minutes. Add some oil to the boiled wheat noodles. Add marinated chicken to the air fryer basket. Cook for about 6 minutes at 393°F after sprinkling oil over it. Cook for another 5 minutes after adding the remainder of the ingredients. Cook for another 5 minutes after adding the noodles. Sprinkle sesame seeds on top and serve.

Nutrients: Kcal 210, Fats: 12g, Total Carbs: 17g, Proteins: 31g

5. Low Carb Chicken Pie

Prep time: 20 minutes

Cook time: 7 minutes

Servings: 4

Ingredients

- Salt
- 1 tsp of soy sauce
- Black pepper
- 1 chopped carrot
- 1 tbsp of cornflour
- 2 sheets puff pastry
- 1/2 tsp of garlic powder
- 1 tbsp of coconut milk
- 1 tbsp of unsalted butter
- 2 chopped mushrooms
- 2 boneless chicken thighs
- 1 chopped yellow onion
- 1 tsp of Italian seasoning
- 1 tsp of Worcestershire sauce

Instructions

Toss the vegetables in a skillet over medium heat until they are soft. Cook for about 3 minutes, stirring occasionally. Toss in all of the other ingredients, except the unsalted butter. Using a pastry sheet, place a layer of dough on the bottom of the air fryer pan. Remove any excess mixture from the corner and spread it on top. Trim the extra sheet from the top and the sides of the pie. Air fry for about 7 minutes at 360°F. Serve and enjoy.

Nutrients: Kcal 300, Fats: 5g, Total Carbs: 14g, Proteins: 7g

6. Chicken Kebabs

Prep time: 10 minutes

Cook time: 20 minutes

Servings: 2

Ingredients

- 1/4 cup of honey
- Cooking spray
- 1/3 cup of soy sauce
- 6 mushrooms, chopped
- 3 bell peppers, diced
- 2 chicken breasts, chopped
- Salt & black pepper, as per taste

Instructions

Combine the chicken, salt, honey, pepper, soy sauce, and oil in a large mixing bowl.

Mash everything together with mushrooms and bell peppers. Make kebabs and air fry for about 20 minutes at 338°F. Serve and enjoy.

Nutrients: Kcal 261, Fats: 7g, Total Carbs: 12g, Proteins: 6g

7. Chicken Nuggets

Prep time: 10 minutes

Cook time: 17 minutes

Servings: 4

Ingredients

- 1 egg
- 1 tsp of sea salt
- 1/2 cup of almond flour
- 1 cup of Greek yogurt
- 1 pack of ranch powder
- 1/2 tsp of black pepper
- 1/4 cup of parmesan cheese
- 1 tsp of smoked paprika
- 1 1/4 lbs of boneless chicken breasts

Instructions

Preheat your air fryer at 390°F. In a large mixing bowl, whisk together the egg and ranch powder; then add the chicken pieces and toss to coat. Mix the almond flour, salt, parmesan cheese, paprika, ranch powder, and pepper in a zip bag until well-combined and crumbly. Add chicken pieces in the coating bag and mix well. Put these in the air fryer basket. Cook for about 17 minutes in the air fryer until golden brown. Make the dipping sauce by combining Greek yogurt and some ranch powder. Serve and enjoy

Nutrients: Kcal 296, Fats: 20g, Total Carbs: 14g, Proteins: 15g

8. Cornish Chicken

Prep time: 10 minutes

Cook time: 25 minutes

Servings: 2

Ingredients

- Salt - Olive oil
- 1 lemon
- 1 Cornish chicken
- Black pepper

Instructions

Preheat the air fryer at390°F. Coat the chicken with olive oil. Squeeze lemon inside it. Add any stuffing if you want. Season it well with salt and pepper. Tie it with a string. Spray the air fryer basket with olive oil. Cook chicken for about 25 minutes until golden brown. Serve and enjoy.

Nutrients: Kcal 566, Fats: 45g, Total Carbs: 0g, Proteins: 50g

9. Cheesy Scotch Eggs

Prep time: 5 minutes

Cook time: 12 minutes

Servings: 2

Ingredients

- 6 eggs
- 3/4 lbs of sausage
- 1/4 cup of parmesan cheese, shredded

Instructions

Preheat the air fryer at 390°F. Boil eggs. Peel eggs and set them aside. Divide sausage into equal portions. Roll sausages with a wrap, and it should look like a small pancake. Wrap the egg in it. Do the same with all eggs. Coat the outer surface with cheese. Put these in an air fryer basket and cook for about 12 minutes. Serve and enjoy.

Nutrients: Kcal 233, Fats: 25g, Total Carbs: 23g, Proteins: 20g

10. Air Fried Chicken Fillets

Prep time: 10 minutes

Cook time: 15 minutes

Servings: 3

Ingredients

- 2 eggs
- 2 tbsp of vegetable oil
- 12 ounces of chicken fillets
- 1/2 teaspoon salt
- 1 tsp of black pepper
- 8 tbsp of breadcrumbs
- 4 ounces of almond flour

Instructions

Preheat the air fryer at 330°F. Mix oil, pepper, and salt in breadcrumbs and mix well. Add chicken fillets into flour and then into egg mixture. Then coat with breadcrumb mixture. Put these into sprayed air fryer basket. Cook for about 15 minutes at 390°F. Serve and enjoy.

Nutrients: Kcal 162, Fats: 4g, Total Carbs: 0g, Proteins: 30g

11. Chicken Drumettes

Prep time: 15 minutes

Cook time: 15 minutes

Servings: 3

Ingredients

- 3/4 tsp of brown sugar
- 1 tsp of sesame oil
- 3 tsp of prawn paste
- 1 tsp of ginger juice
- 1/2 tsp of Shaoxing wine
- 1/2 ounces of chicken drumettes
- 6 tsp of vegetable oil

Instructions

Mix the brown sugar, sesame oil, wine, ginger juice, and prawn paste to form the marinade. Marinate chicken overnight in the fridge. Preheat the air fryer for about 5 minutes at 356°F. Spray chicken with vegetable oil and place in air fryer basket. Cook for about 7 minutes, turn the drumettes over and cook for another 8 minutes until golden. Serve and enjoy.

Nutrients: Kcal 90, Fats: 7g, Total Carbs: 3g, Proteins: 5g

12. Fried Chicken Popcorns

Prep time: 20 minutes

Cook time: 15 minutes

Servings: 2

Ingredients

- 1 egg
- Breadcrumbs
- 1 cup of corn starch
- 1/4 cup of water
- 1 tbsp of soy sauce
- 1/4 tsp of five-spice
- 1/4 tsp of pepper
- 1/2 tsp of potato starch
- 1 clove of garlic, minced
- 1/4 tsp of chili pepper
- 2 green onions, minced
- 1 lb of chicken breast, boneless

Instructions

Chop chicken into cubes. Add minced garlic and onion to a small bowl. Mix well, and then add all the spices. Mix well. Coat chicken with this mixture. Marinate for about 30 minutes. Preheat the air fryer to 390°F. Beat egg with water in a bowl, add corn starch, and mix well. Coat chicken cubes with starch. Cook in the air fryer for about 12 minutes. Serve and enjoy.

Nutrients: Kcal 170, Fats: 7g, Total Carbs: 14g, Proteins: 14g

13. Herbal Chicken and Sweet Potatoes

Prep time: 5 minutes

Cook time: 23 minutes

Servings: 2

Ingredients

- 1 sweet potato
- 1 tsp of olive oil
- Salad greens
- 1/2 portion of chicken, halved
- 1 tbsp of herbs chicken spices

Instructions

Marinate chicken with olive oil and herb spices for an hour in the fridge. Cook sweet potato in the air fryer for about 10 minutes at 350°F. Then cook marinated chicken pieces in the air fryer for 12 minutes until golden brown. Serve with salad greens and enjoy.

Nutrients: Kcal 220, Fats: 7g, Total Carbs: 18g, Proteins: 16g

14. Saucy Chicken Wingettes

Prep time: 40 minutes

Cook time: 25 minutes

Servings: 6

Ingredients

- 1 1/2 ounces of honey
- 1/2 tsp of pepper
- 1 tsp of soy sauce
- 3 tsp of oyster sauce
- 20 chicken wingettes
- 1 cup of Chinese wine
- 1 1/2 ounces of canola oil

Instructions

Mix all the ingredients to make the marinade. Marinate chicken for about 30 minutes. Heat the air fryer to 392°F. Cook the chicken for about 15 minutes. Once done, turn it and cook for about 10 minutes until golden brown. Serve and enjoy.

Nutrients: Kcal 200, Fats: 8g, Total Carbs: 15g, Proteins: 19g

15. Healthy Sausage Mix

Prep time: 10 minutes

Cook time: 10 minutes

Servings: 4

Ingredients

- 2 tbsp of mustard
- 1 bell pepper. diced
- 1/3 cup of ketchup
- 1/2 cup of chicken stock
- 3 tbsp of brown sugar
- 1/2 cup of chopped onion
- 1 pound of sliced sausages
- 2 tbsp of apple cider vinegar

Instructions

Mix all the ingredients in a bowl. Pour in the pan of the air fryer and cook for about 10 minutes at 350°F. Serve and enjoy.

Nutrients: Kcal 162, Fats: 6g, Total Carbs: 12g, Proteins: 6g

16. Nutty Chicken

Prep time: 10 minutes

Cook time: 17 minutes

Servings: 4

Ingredients

- 2 cups of basil - 4 zucchinis, diced
- 1/2 cup of olive oil
- 3/4 cup of pine nuts
- 3 minced garlic cloves
- 2 cups of chopped kale
- Salt & black pepper

- 1 tbsp of lemon juice
- 1/2 cup of chopped almonds
- 2 cups of cherry tomatoes, halved
- 1 pound of chicken breasts, chopped

Instructions

Blend kale and basil in a bowl. Add nuts, salt, olive oil, garlic, and lemon juice in a bowl and mix well. Saute some garlic in a pan. Add all other ingredients except chicken for pesto and stir. Mix well with chicken pieces. Cook in the air fryer for around 17 minutes at 360°F. Serve and enjoy.

Nutrients: Kcal 344, Fats: 8g, Total Carbs: 12g, Proteins: 16g

17. Healthy Chicken Casserole

Prep time: 20 minutes

Cook time: 17 minutes

Servings: 6

Ingredients

- 1 cup of salsa
- Cooking spray
- 2 tsp of chili powder
- 2 tsp of ground cumin
- 1 tbsp of garlic powder
- 6 chopped kale leaves
- 1 cup of tomato sauce
- 1/2 cup of chopped cilantro
- 10 ounces of sweet corn
- 1 cup of quinoa, cooked
- 2 chopped jalapeno peppers
- 1/2 cup of chopped green onions
- 12 ounces of black beans, canned
- 3 cups of mozzarella cheese, grated
- 3 cups of boiled chicken breast, shredded

Instructions

Spray dish with cooking spray and all ingredients in it. Mix well. Cook in the air fryer for about 17 minutes at 350°F. Serve and enjoy.

Nutrients: Kcal 365, Fats: 12g, Total Carbs: 22g, Proteins: 26g

18. Air Fried Turkish Chicken

Prep time: 10 minutes

Cook time: 40 minutes

Servings: 4

Ingredients

- 1 tbsp of tomato paste
- 1/2 tsp of black pepper
- 1/2 tsp of cayenne pepper
- 1/4 cup of Greek yogurt
- 1 tbsp of vegetable oil
- 1 tsp of kosher salt
- 1/2 tsp of cinnamon
- 1 tsp of ground cumin
- 1 tbsp of lemon juice
- 1 tbsp of minced garlic
- 1 tsp of smoked paprika
- 1 lb of boneless chicken, diced

Instructions

Mix everything and coat chicken pieces with it. Marinate for about 30 minutes. Cook each side of chicken in the air fryer for about 10 minutes at 370°F. Serve and enjoy.

Nutrients: Kcal 298, Fast: 23g, Total Carbs: 4g, Proteins: 20g

19. Cheesy Chicken Wings

Prep time: 10 minutes

Cook time: 15 minutes

Servings: 4

Ingredients

- 1 tsp of paprika
- 2 lbs of chicken wings
- Salt as per taste - Cooking spray
- 1/2 cup of Parmesan cheese, grated

Instructions

Mix everything in a small bowl. Add chicken and coat with mixture. Cook in the air fryer for about 15 minutes at 350°F. Garnish with herbs and parmesan cheese. Serve and enjoy.

Nutrients: Kcal 328, Fats: 23g, Total Carbs: 11g, Proteins: 27g

20. Garlic Chicken Wings

Prep time: 8 minutes

Cook time: 30 minutes

Servings: 6

Ingredients

- 1 tsp of salt - 2 lb of chicken wings
- 1 tsp of parsley - 2 tbsp of minced garlic - 1/4 tsp of pepper
- 3/4 cup of Parmesan cheese, grated

Instructions

Mix all ingredients in a bowl. Mix wings in it. Cook wings in the air fryer for about 28 minutes at 400°F. Flip and cook for about 12 minutes. Serve with ketchup and enjoy.

Nutrients: Kcal 350, Fats: 23g, Total Carbs: 11g, Proteins: 37g

21. Healthy Egg Bites

Prep time: 10 minutes

Cook time: 12 minutes

Servings: 8

Ingredients

- 6 eggs - 3 tbsp of bacon
- Cooking spray
- 3 tbsp of whole milk - 1/2 tsp of salt
- 1/4 tsp of black pepper - 2 tbsp of scallions
- 1/4 cup of cheddar cheese

Instructions

Spray the mold with cooking spray. Mix everything in a large bowl. Pour this mixture into molds. Set it into an air fryer and cook for about 12 minutes at 350°F. Serve and enjoy.

Nutrients: Kcal 83, Fats: 5g, Total Carbs: 2g, Proteins: 8g

22. Chicken Tacos

Prep time: 10 minutes

Cook time: 12 minutes

Servings: 4

Ingredients

For Taco Mixture

- 1 egg
- 1 tsp of paprika
- 1 1/2 tsp of salt
- Cooking oil spray
- 3 tbsp of buttermilk
- 1/2 tsp of onion powder
- 1/2 tsp of black pepper
- 1 tsp of garlic powder
- 1 lb of chicken tenders
- 3 tbsp of corn starch
- 3/4 cup of cornflour
- 1/2 tsp of cayenne pepper

For Coleslaw

- 1/2 tsp of salt
- 1 tbsp of water
- 2 cups of coleslaw mix
- 1 tbsp of brown sugar
- 1/4 tsp of pepper flakes
- 2 tbsp of apple cider vinegar

For Mayo

- 1/2 tsp of salt
- 1 tsp of garlic powder
- 2 tbsp of hot sauce
- 1/4 cup of mayo
- 1 tbsp of buttermilk

Instructions

Mix brown sugar, vinegar, salt, coleslaw, pepper flakes, and water in a bowl. Set it aside. Mix mayo, hot sauce, buttermilk, garlic powder, and salt in another bowl. Preheat the air fryer to 360°F. Mix egg, salt, pepper, and buttermilk in a bowl. Mix cornflour, corn starch, onion powder, garlic powder, salt, cayenne pepper, and black pepper in another bowl. Cut tenders into small pieces and season with salt and pepper. Dip these into the egg mixture and then into the flour mixture. Cook in the air fryer for about 10 minutes at 360°F, turning halfway through. Take these out and put them in tortilla shells. Serve with coleslaw and mayo.

Nutrients: Kcal 389, Fats: 15g, Total Carbs: 31g, Proteins: 29g

23. Fried Chicken Rice

Prep time: 10 minutes

Cook time: 5 minutes

Servings: 4

Ingredients

- 6 tbsp of soy sauce
- 4 cups of white rice
- 1 cup of chicken breast
- 1/4 cup of carrots, chopped
- 1/4 cup of celery, chopped
- Cooking spray
- 1/4 cup of onion, chopped

Instructions

Spray air fryer basket and line with foil. Add all the ingredients in it and mix well. Cook in the air fryer at 390°F for about 5 minutes. Add soy sauce after some time and cook for 5 more minutes. Serve and enjoy.

Nutrients: Kcal 350, Fats: 6g, Total Carbs: 52g, Proteins: 22g

24. Gluten-Free Chicken Bites

Prep time: 10 minutes

Cook time: 12 minutes

Servings: 4

Ingredients

- 2 eggs
- Parsley
- 1 lemon
- 1/2 cup of gluten-free flour
- 5 tbsp of olive oil
- 1 cup of gluten-free breadcrumbs
- 5 chicken breast fillets
- 1/2 cup of whole egg mayo
- 1 tsp of sriracha

Instructions

Preheat the air fryer for 3 minutes at 200°F. Mix breadcrumbs and parsley in a small bowl. Whisk egg in another bowl. Dip chicken in egg mixture and then coat with breadcrumbs. Line the air fryer basket with parchment paper. Cook chicken bites for about 12 minutes. Mix sriracha, spices, and mayo to make the sauce. Garnish the bites with parsley and serve with sauce.

Nutrients: Kcal 415, Fats: 32.7g, Total Carbs: 24.5g, Proteins: 8.3g

25. Chicken with Citrus Sauce

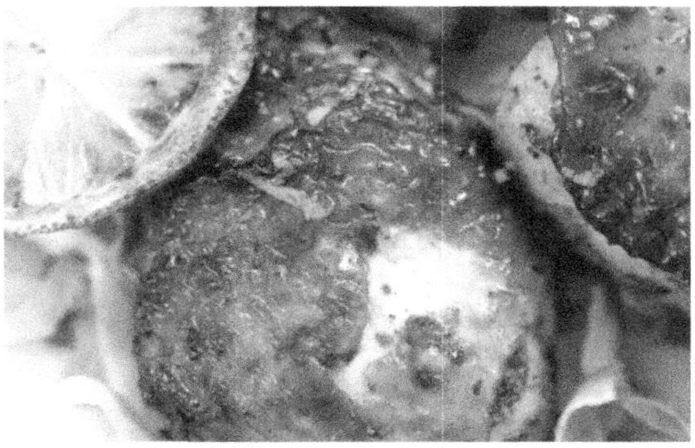

Prep time: 10 minutes

Cook time: 12 minutes

Servings: 4

Ingredients

- 2 tbsp of water
- 1 orange zest
- 2 tsp of cornstarch
- 1 tsp of soy sauce
- 2 tbsp of cornstarch
- 1/2 cup of orange juice
- 2 tbsp of brown sugar
- 1 tsp of rice wine vinegar
- 1 tsp of ground ginger
- Red pepper flakes
- 1 pound of boneless chicken breasts

Instructions

Preheat the air fryer to 400°F. Coat chicken with cornstarch. Cook for 9 minutes in the air fryer. Mix and cook all the other ingredients in a pan to make the sauce. Add cornstarch and water in it and cook for about 5 more minutes. Serve chicken with sauce and enjoy.

Nutrients: Kcal 630, Fats: 15g, Total Carbs: 46g, Proteins: 75g

CHAPTER 8:

Meat Recipes

1. Meatloaf

Prep time: 10 minutes

Cook time: 40 minutes

Servings: 6

Ingredients

- 2 eggs - 1 tsp of garlic salt
- 1 cup of ketchup - 2 lbs of ground beef
- 1/2 cup of onion
- 1/4 cup of parley
- 1/4 cup of whole milk
- 3/4 cup of breadcrumbs
- 1 tsp of Italian seasoning
- 1 tbsp of Worcestershire sauce
- 1/2 cup of brown sugar
- 1 tbsp of ground mustard

Instructions

Mix the eggs, crumbs, and whole milk in a large bowl. Mix all the other ingredients in another bowl. Line the loaf pan with parchment paper. Add the mixture to it. Cook in the air fryer at 370°F for about 30 minutes. Mix ketchup, mustard, and brown sugar in a bowl to make the sauce. Pour sauce over the top of the meatloaf. Cook for another 15 minutes. Serve and enjoy.

Nutrients: Kcal 563, Fats: 33g, Total Carbs: 36g, Proteins: 30g

2. Healthy Ribeye Steak

Prep time: 10 minutes

Cook time: 15 minutes

Servings: 1

Ingredients

- 1 tsp of salt
- 1 rib-eye steak
- 1 tbsp of olive oil
- 1 tsp of black pepper
- 1 tbsp of steak seasoning

Instructions

Preheat the air fryer for about 3 minutes at 400°F. Rub olive oil over steak. Season both sides with salt, seasoning, and pepper. Cook steak in the air fryer for about 8 minutes. Serve and enjoy.

Nutrients: Kcal 594, Fats: 46g, Total Carbs: 6g, Proteins: 45g

3. Bacon Sandwiches

Prep time: 10 minutes

Cook time: 15 minutes

Servings: 4

Ingredients

- 1/3 cup of bbq sauce
- 2 tbsp of honey
- 2 tomatoes
- 8 slices of bacon
- 1 red bell pepper
- 3 pita pockets, halved
- 1 1/4 cup of lettuce leaves
- 1 sliced yellow bell pepper

Instructions

Mix everything except pita pockets, tomatoes, and lettuce in a bowl. Then cook in the air fryer for about 5 minutes at 350°F. Stuff this bacon mixture, tomatoes, and lettuce in pita pockets. Serve with bbq sauce and enjoy.

Nutrients: Kcal 186, Fats: 6g, Total Carbs: 14g, Proteins: 4g

4. Beef Cubes

Prep time: 10 minutes

Cook time: 13 minutes

Servings: 4

Ingredients

- White rice, cooked
- 1 pound of sirloin
- 2 tbsp of olive oil
- 16 ounces of pasta sauce
- 1 1/2 cups of breadcrumbs
- 1/2 tsp of marjoram, dried

Instructions

Marinate beef cubes with pasta sauce. Mix oil, crumbs, and dried marjoram in another bowl. Coat beef cubes with this mixture. Cook these cubes in the air fryer for around 12 minutes at 360°F. Serve with white rice.

Nutrients: Kcal 271, Fats: 6g, Total Carbs: 18g, Proteins: 12g

5. Garlic Bacon Pizza

Prep time: 10 minutes

Cook time: 13 minutes

Servings: 4

Ingredients

- Cooking spray
- 4 dinner rolls
- 1 cup of tomato sauce
- 4 garlic cloves, minced
- 1/2 tsp of garlic powder
- 6 bacon slices, chopped
- 1/2 tsp of oregano, dried
- 1 1/4 cups of cheddar cheese, shredded

Instructions

Spray dinner rolls and place them in the air fryer. Cook for around 2 minutes at 370°F. Add all the ingredients on top and cook again for around 8 minutes at 370°F. Serve and enjoy.

Nutrients: Kcal 217, Fats: 5g, Total Carbs: 12g, Proteins: 4g

6. Mexican Pizza

Prep time: 15 minutes

Cook time: 13 minutes

Servings: 2

Ingredients

- 4 tortillas - Green onions
- Sour cream
- 2 tbsp of olive oil
- 15 ounces of beans
- 1/4 cup of salsa
- Olives, sliced
- 1/2 lb of ground beef
- 1 tomato, chopped
- Shredded lettuce
- 5 ounces of enchilada
- 1 cup of cheddar cheese, grated
- 1 pack of taco seasoning

Instructions

Make taco beef as per instructions on the pack. Grease the tortillas and fry for about 2 minutes at 370°F. Top with beans, salsa, and taco beef. Add another tortilla on top of it. Sprinkle cheese, tomatoes, and olives on top. Cook for around 3 minutes at 370°F. Serve and enjoy.

Nutrients: Kcal 648, Fats: 13g, Total Carbs: 49g, Proteins: 34g

7. Beef Meatballs

Prep time: 15 minutes

Cook time: 15 minutes

Servings: 4

Ingredients

- 1/2 lb of ground beef Mashed potatoes - 1/2 tsp of garlic powder
- 1/2 tsp of onion powder
- Salt & black pepper, as per taste
- 1/2 cup of grated cheddar cheese
- 1/2 pound of chopped Italian sausage

Instructions

Mix all the ingredients and make small balls. Cook in the air fryer for around 15 minutes at 370°F. Serve with mashed potatoes.

Nutrients: Kcal 333, Fats: 23g, Total Carbs: 8g, Proteins: 20g

8. Avocado and Beef Bombs

Prep time: 20 minutes

Cook time: 45 minutes

Servings: 2

Ingredients

- 2 avocados
- 1 lb of ground beef
- 6 pieces of bacon
- 2 tbsp of diced onions
- 2 tbsp of diced jalapenos
- 1/2 cup of cheddar cheese, shredded

Instructions

Cut avocados in half and fill them with shredded cheese. Seal with another avocado half. Mix beef, jalapenos, and onions in a bowl. Then press it over the avocado pieces. Wrap avocadoes with bacon slices. Cook in the air fryer for about 40 minutes at 350°F. Serve and enjoy.

Nutrients: Kcal 1323, Fats: 91g, Total Carbs: 21g, Proteins: 84g

9. Beefy Peppers

Prep time: 15 minutes

Cook time: 15 minutes

Servings: 2

Ingredients

- 2 tbsp of olive oil
- Cilantro and lime cream
- 1 cup of tomato sauce
- 1 green pepper, chopped
- 1 tsp of taco seasoning
- 1 pound of ground meat
- 1/2 cup of cheddar cheese

Instructions

Spray peppers with olive oil and cook in the air fryer for about 5 minutes at 400°F. Cook meat with tomato sauce and seasoning in a pan. Fill peppers with this meat mixture. Cook in the air fryer for about 5 minutes at 330°F. Sprinkle cheese on top. Use cilantro and lime cream for dressing it. Serve and enjoy.

Nutrients: Kcal: 560, Fats: 41g, Total Carbs: 19g, Proteins: 30g

10. Spinach Beef Pinwheels

Prep time: 5 minutes

Cook time: 15 minutes

Servings: 2

Ingredients

- 1 pound of beef steak
- Salt and pepper to taste
- 1/4 cup of garlic cream cheese
- 10 ounces of frozen spinach

Instructions

Season steak with cream cheese, salt, pepper, and spinach.

Wrap and set aside. Preheat the air fryer for about 5 minutes at 400°F.

Then cook steaks in it for 6 minutes on each side. Serve and enjoy.

Nutrients: Kcal: 760, Fats: 56g, Total Carbs: 78g, Proteins: 78g

11. Nutritious Lamb Steak

Prep time: 35 minutes

Cook time: 15 minutes

Servings: 4

Ingredients

- 1/2 Onion
- 4 slices of ginger
- 5 cloves of garlic
- 1 tsp of garam masala
- 1 tsp of ground fennel
- 1 tsp of cinnamon
- 1/2 tsp of cardamom
- 1 tsp of cayenne Pepper
- 1 tsp of kosher salt
- 1 pound of lamb boneless steaks

Instructions

Blend everything except the steak using a blender for around 4 minutes.

Add steak to a bowl and slash the meat with the help of the knife.

Add the paste and let it rest for at least 30 minutes.

Place it in the air fryer basket in one layer and cook for around 15 minutes at 330°F. Serve and enjoy.

Nutrients: Kcal 182, Fats: 7g, Total Carbs: 3g, Proteins: 24g

12. Cheesy Steak

Prep time: 15 minutes

Cook time: 15 minutes

Servings: 7

Ingredients

- 32 ounces of Rib-eye steaks
- 2 tsp of kosher salt
- 1.5 tsp of black pepper
- 4 ounces of low-fat cheese
- 1 tsp of garlic powder
- 4 ounces of unsalted butter

Instructions

Add all the ingredients to a bowl and mash with a fork. Cover and place in the fridge for around 15 minutes to get firm. Coat steaks using pepper, garlic powder, and salt. Place steaks in the basket and cook for around 4 minutes at 400°F. Flip and cook for 3 more minutes. Top with butter and enjoy.

Nutrition: Kcal 829, Fats: 60g, Total Carbs: 2g, Proteins: 69g

13. Turkey Breast

Prep time: 2 hours

Cook time: 1 hour

Servings: 8

Ingredients

- 2 tsp of olive oil
- 1 turkey breast
- 1/2 cup of cooking oil
- 1/2 tsp of kosher salt
- 1/2 tsp o black pepper
- 1/2 tsp of garlic - 1/2 tsp of onion
- 1 tsp of powder dark chili

For Brine

- 1 carrot
- 1/2 gallon of cold water
- 1/4 cup of kosher salt
- 1/4 cup of brown sugar
- 3 cloves garlic, halved
- 1 tbsp of black peppercorns
- 1 quartered yellow onion
- 1/4 bunch of fresh parsley
- A few bay leaves

Instructions

Boil water in a pot. Mix brown sugar and salt in it. Take off the flame and mix the rest of the ingredients in it. Allow it to cool. Put turkey in the mixture and place in the fridge for around 2 hours. Rub oil after drying the breast. Season using spices and salt. Warm half cup of cooking oil in a pan. Cook turkey in the air fryer for around 50 minutes at 400°F. Serve and enjoy.

Nutrients: Kcal 160, Fats: 4g, Total Carbs: 9g, Proteins: 21g

14. Rosemary Beef

Prep time: 10 minutes

Cook time: 40 minutes

Servings: 6

Ingredients

- 2 lb of beef roast
- 1 tbsp of olive oil
- 2 tsp of thyme
- 1 tsp of salt
- 2 tsp of rosemary

Instructions

Mix rosemary, oil, and sea salt on a plate. Coat beef with the mixture on the plate. Place in the basket and cook for around 10 minutes at 390°F. Cook for 30 more minutes at 360°F. Serve and enjoy.

Nutrients: Kcal 212, Fats: 7g, Total Carbs: 2g, Proteins: 33g

15. Low-Carb Lamb Burgers

Prep time: 10 minutes

Cook time: 18 minutes

Servings: 4

Ingredient

- 1 tbsp of Moroccan spice
- 1 lb of minced lamb
- Salt & Pepper
- 2 tsp of garlic puree
- 1 tsp of harissa paste

Greek Dip

- 3 tbsp of Greek yogurt
- 1 tsp of Moroccan spice
- 1/2 tsp of oregano
- 1 Lemon juice

Instructions

Place all ingredients in a bowl and mix. Shape the mince using burger press into circular shapes. Cook in the air fryer for around 18 minutes at 360°F. Mix dip ingredients in the meantime in a bowl. Serve with burgers.

Nutrients: Kcal 478, Fats: 38g, Total Carbs: 3g, Proteins: 28g

16. Herb Flavored Lamb

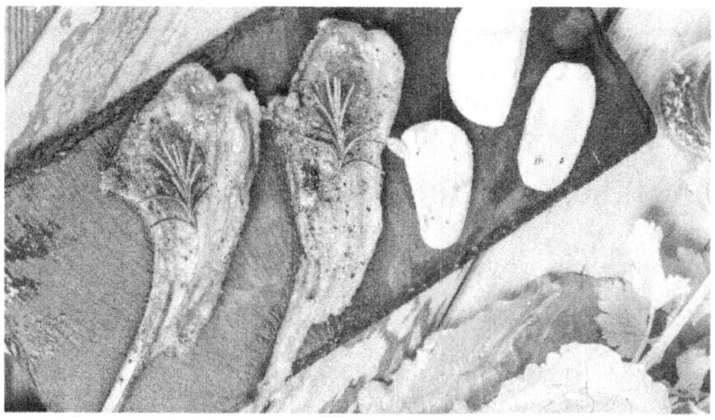

Prep time: 10 minutes

Cook time: 10 minutes

Servings: 4

Ingredients

- salt
- 1 rack of lamb
- pepper
- 2 tbsp of dried rosemary
- 1 tbsp of dried thyme
- 4 tbsp of olive oil
- 2 tsp of minced garlic

Instructions

Mix herbs in a bowl along with oil. Mix and coat lamb with it. Place in the air fryer and cook for around 10 minutes at 360°F. Serve and enjoy.

Nutrients: Kcal 346, Fats: 11g, Total Carbs: 23g, Proteins: 34g

17. Healthy Steak Kababs

Prep time: 50 minutes

Cook time: 10 minutes

Servings: 4

Ingredients

- 1 red onion, diced
- 1 lb. of sirloin steak, diced
- 1 bell pepper, diced

For the Marinade

- 1 tsp of minced garlic
- 2 tbsp of olive oil
- 1 tsp of black pepper
- 1/4 cup of soy sauce
- 1 tsp of grated ginger
- 2 tbsp of red wine vinegar

Instructions

Mix all the marinade ingredients in a small bowl. Then add steak, onion, and bell pepper to it. Keep in the fridge for a few hours. Use skewers to thread everything. Make kababs with the mixture. Cook in the air fryer at 350°F for about 10 minutes. Serve and enjoy.

Nutrients: Kcal 366, Fats: 23g, Total Carbs: 6g, Proteins: 33g

18. Beef with Broccoli

Prep time: 5 minutes

Cook time: 10 minutes

Servings: 10

Ingredients

- 1 pack of Frozen beef cubes
- Olive oil spray
- 1 pack of frozen broccoli
- Any sauce

Instructions

Add everything to a bowl and mix well. Grease the air fryer basket. Cook at 370°F for about 10 minutes. Add sauce and serve.

Nutrients: Kcal 165, Fats: 10g, Total Carbs: 7g, Proteins: 7g

19. Beef Salad

Prep time: 10 minutes

Cook time: 20 minutes

Servings: 2

Ingredients

- 1 lb of lean beef - 1 tsp of salt
- 1/2 tsp of black pepper
- 1 tomato, sliced
- 15 ounces of black beans
- 1 scallion, sliced
- 1/2 tsp of chili spice blend
- 2 tsp of olive oil

- 1 head of lettuce
- 1/2 cup of corn
- 8 corn tortillas

For the Dressing

- 1 cup of fresh cilantro
- 1 tsp of honey - 1/4 tsp of salt
- 1/4 cup of olive oil
- 1/8 cup of lime juice
- 1/1 tsp of minced garlic
- 1/2 tsp of ground coriander

Instructions

Saute beef and beans. Add spices and sauce. Coat tortillas with olive oil. Put in the air fryer and cook for 4 minutes at 340°F. Assemble everything in a bowl. Make the dressing by mixing all the dressing ingredients. Pour dressing over the salad and enjoy.

Nutrients: Kcal 350, Fats: 34g, Total Carbs: 70g, Proteins: 80g

20. Salami Bites

Prep time: 5 minutes

Cook time: 5 minutes

Servings: 10

Ingredients

- Filling
- Olive oil
- Spices
- 10 pieces of salami

Instructions

Place salami pieces on each other in the ramekin. Cook in the air fryer for about 4 minutes at 400°F. Let it cool, and then add filling to it. Enjoy.

Nutrients: Kcal 217, Fats: 14g, Total Carbs: 15g, Proteins: 7g

21. Beefy Stir Fry

Prep time: 20 minutes

Cook time: 10 minutes

Servings: 2

Ingredients

- 1 lb of beef sirloin, diced
- 1 cup of red pepper, diced
- 1 cup of yellow pepper, diced
- 1 1/2 lbs of broccoli florets
- 1/2 cup of onions, chopped
- 1 cup of green pepper, diced
- 1/2 cup of red onion, chopped

For the Marinade

- 1/4 cup water
- 1 tsp of sesame oil
- 1/4 cup hoisin sauce
- 1 tbsp of soy sauce
- 2 tsp of minced garlic
- 1 tsp of ground ginger

Instructions

Mix all the marinade ingredients in a bowl. Marinade the meat and keep it in the fridge for about 20 minutes. Cook vegetables in the air fryer for about 5 minutes at 200°F. Then cook meat in the air fryer for about 5 minutes at 360°F. Serve it with brown rice and enjoy.

Nutrients: Kcal 149, Fats: 2g, Total Carbs: 30g, Proteins: 8g

22. Korean Beef

Prep time: 20 minutes

Cook time: 30 minutes

Servings: 6

Ingredients

- Coconut oil spray
- 1 lb of flank steak
- 1/2 cup of brown sugar
- 1/4 cup of cornstarch
- 1 tsp of ground ginger
- 1/2 cup of soy sauce, gluten-free
- 1 tbsp of chili sauce
- 2 tbsp of white wine vinegar
- 1 clove garlic, minced
- 1/2 tsp of sesame seeds
- 1 tbsp of water

Instructions

Mix steak pieces and cornstarch. Line the air fryer basket with foil. Cook steak pieces for about 20 minutes at 390°F. Add all the other ingredients to a pan to make the sauce. Pour this sauce over the meat and serve with rice or beans.

Nutrients: Kcal 489, Fats: 22g, Total Carbs: 32g, Proteins: 38g

23. Beef Meatballs

Prep time: 10 minutes

Cook time: 15 minutes

Servings: 4

Ingredients

- 1/2 tsp of onion powder
- 1/2 pound of ground beef
- 1/2 tsp of garlic powder
- Salt & black, pepper as per taste
- 1/2 cup of fat-free cheese
- Green beans
- 1/2 pound of chopped Italian sausage

Instructions

Mix all the ingredients in a bowl and make balls. Place them in the fryer and cook for around 15 minutes at 370°F. Serve with green beans.

Nutrients: Kcal 333, Fats: 23g, Total Carbs: 8g, Proteins: 20g

24. Steak with Cabbage

Prep time: 10 minutes

Cook time: 10 minutes

Servings: 4

Ingredients

- 2 tsp of cornstarch
- 1 tbsp of peanut oil
- 1 chopped yellow bell pepper
- 2 chopped green onions
- 2 minced garlic cloves
- Salt & black pepper, as per taste
- 2 cups of chopped green cabbage
- 1/2 pound of sirloin steak, diced

Instructions

Mix cabbage, peanut oil, black pepper, and salt in a bowl. Place in the basket and cook for around 5 minutes at 370°F. Add steak to the air fryer and mix the rest of the ingredients. Cook for around 5 minutes. Serve with cabbage.

Nutrients: Kcal 282, Fats: 6g, Total Carbs: 14g, Proteins: 6g

25. Creamy Beef

Prep time: 10 minutes

Cook time: 10 minutes

Servings: 6

Ingredients

- 3 tsp of butter, unsalted
- 3 beef sausages
- 1/2 cup of creamy sauce
- 4 crushed cloves of garlic
- 6 tsp of cubed carrot
- 11/2 ounces of low-fat cheese, grated
- 2 cups of cooked rice
- 11/2 ounces of broccoli florets

Instructions

Melt butter in a pan and cook garlic for around 2 minutes. Add broccoli and carrots and cook for 4 more minutes. Add sausage and cook for around 3 minutes. Stir creamy sauce and rice in it. Spread cheese on top and cook in the air fryer for around 10 minutes at 356°F.

Nutrients: Kcal 222, Fats: 9g, Total Carbs: 16g, Proteins: 27g

CHAPTER 9:

Dessert Recipes

1. Chocolate Protein Balls

Prep time: 20 minutes

Cook time: 15 minutes

Servings: 10

Ingredients

- 1 cup of oats
- 2 tbsp of chia seeds
- 1/3 cup of honey
- 1 tbsp of protein powder
- 2 tbsp of flax seeds
- 1/2 cup of peanut butter
- 1/4 cup of dark chocolate, chopped

Instructions

Mix all the ingredients in a bowl. Put it in the refrigerator for about 30 minutes. After that, spray some oil on the air fryer basket and place the balls in it. Cook in the air fryer for about 10 minutes at 325°F. Serve and enjoy.

Nutrients: Kcal 188, Fats: 9.9g, Total Carbs: 21.5g, Proteins: 5.8g

2. Caramel Pineapple Rings

Prep time: 10 minutes

Cook time: 10 minutes

Servings: 10

Ingredients

- A pinch of sea salt
- 4 tbsp of brown sugar
- 2 tbsp of butter, melted
- 1 can of Pineapple rings

Instructions

Put the pineapple rings in the air fryer basket. Add butter and sugar mixture over the top of rings and spread evenly. Air fry these at 380°F for about 10 minutes. Sprinkle some sea salt and brown sugar on top. Cook at 400°F for about 4 minutes until it gets brown. Enjoy.

Nutrients: Kcal 65, Fats: 2g, Total Carbs: 12g, Proteins: 0g

3. Berry Yogurt Cake

Prep time: 15 minutes

Cook time: 60 minutes

Servings: 12

Ingredients

- 2 eggs
- 1 lemon
- 1 cup of berries
- 1/2 tsp of salt
- 1 1/2 tsp of baking powder
- 1 1/2 cups of cake flour
- 1/4 tsp of baking soda
- 1 cup of brown sugar
- 1/2 tsp of vanilla extract

- 1/2 cup of olive oil
- 1/2 cup of Greek yogurt
- 3 tbsp of lemon juice

Instructions

Add all the ingredients except baking powder, soda, salt, and flour in a separate bowl and whisk together until smooth. Then add the salt, baking powder, soda, and flour and combine well. Add olive oil and whisk until well combined. Add mixed berries. Preheat the air fryer at 300°F. Grease pan with oil. Add the batter in it. Cook in the air fryer for about 60 minutes. Then, slice and serve.

Nutrients: Kcal 291, Fats: 10g, Total Carbs: 44g, Proteins: 5g

4. Pumpkin Bites

Prep time: 15 minutes

Cook time: 10 minutes

Servings: 12

Ingredients

- 1/2 tsp of salt
- 1/2 cup of pumpkin puree
- 2 cups of almond flour
- 1/2 cup of brown sugar
- 1/4 cup of fat-free cream
- 1/2 cup of unsalted butter
- 1 tsp of vanilla extract
- 2 tsp of baking powder
- 1 1/2 tsp of pumpkin pie spice

Instructions

Preheat the air fryer at 400°F. Mix the pumpkin pie spice, brown sugar, butter, salt, almond flour, and baking powder in a food processor. Put in the vanilla extract, cream, and pumpkin puree. Mix until a dough forms.

Roll out the dough. Then, cut into bite-size pieces, and brush milk over them. Cook in air fryer basket at 400°F for about 10 minutes. Serve and enjoy with your loved ones.

Nutrients: Kcal 202, Fats: 10g, Total Carbs: 26g, Proteins: 2g

5. Sugar-free Souffle

Prep time: 15 minutes

Cook time: 12 minutes

Servings: 2

Ingredients

- 2 tbsp of Splenda
- 2 egg whites, 1 egg yolk
- 1/2 tsp of cream
- 1 cup of brown sugar
- 1/3 cup of coconut milk
- 1 tbsp of almond flour
- 1/2 tsp of vanilla extract
- 2 tbsp of melted butter
- 1/4 cup of sugar-free chocolate chips

Instructions

Grease ramekins with melted butter. Sprinkle brown sugar over them. Preheat the air fryer at 325°F. Then, melt the chocolate and butter separately in the microwave. Whisk the almond flour in butter and whisk until it is thick. Add melted chocolate and blend. Put the egg whites and cream in a stand mixer. Whisk the egg whites to form peaks. Then, add the remaining brown sugar, vanilla extract, and egg yolks. Stop whisking when the peak comes, add the egg whites, and mix with the other ingredients. Add the batter in ramekins. Place them in the air fryer. Cook for about 12 minutes. Serve and enjoy.

Nutrients: Kcal 288, Fats: 24g, Total Carbs: 5g, Proteins: 6g

6. Healthy Hazelnut Turnovers

Prep time: 10 minutes

Cook time: 7 minutes

Servings: 12

Ingredients

- 1 egg
- 1 tbsp of water
- 3 tbsp of chopped hazelnuts
- 1 cup of powdered brown sugar
- 1 puff pastry sheet
- 1/3 cup of chocolate-hazelnut spread

Instructions

Preheat the air fryer at 400°F. Roll the puff pastry into a rectangle shape. Cut into small pieces. Put some chocolate hazelnut spread in the center of every piece. Sprinkle some hazelnuts on top. Fold into a triangle. Brush the egg mixture on top and seal completely. Put the turnovers in the air fryer. Cook for about 7 minutes. Top with powdered brown sugar and enjoy.

Nutrients: Kcal 144, Fats: 9g, Total Carbs: 14g, Proteins: 3g

7. Peanut Butter Cookies

Prep time: 10 minutes

Cook time: 7 minutes

Servings: 10

Ingredients

- 1 egg - 1/2 tsp of salt
- 1/2 cup of butter
- 2 tbsp of coconut milk
- 3/4 tsp of baking soda
- 1 cup of brown sugar
- 1/2 cup of peanut butter
- 3/4 cup of all-purpose flour

Instructions

Mix flour and baking soda in a bowl and set it aside. Mix butter and peanut butter in another bowl. Mix milk and egg. Add the flour mixture slowly and combine well until a dough forms. Make balls from the dough. Flatten the cookie. Put cookies in the air fryer basket and cook for about 7 minutes at 350°F. Serve and enjoy.

Per serving: Kcal 355, Fats: 18g, Total Carbs: 45g, Proteins: 6g

8. Maple and Pecan Bars

Prep time: 15 minutes

Cook time: 15 minutes

Servings: 8

Ingredients

- Cooking spray
- 1/4 tsp of sea salt
- 1 1/2 cup of pecans
- 1/4 cup of whole milk
- 1 cup of butter, unsalted
- 1/4 tsp vanilla extract
- 1/4 tsp of kosher salt
- 1/4 cup of maple syrup
- 1/4 cup of brown sugar
- 1 cup of all-purpose flour
- 1/2 cup of brown sugar

Instructions

Place a foil paper in the air fryer basket. Spray some oil on it. Mix butter and brown sugar in a bowl. Then mix the flour and salt into the bowl. Place the mixture in a pan. Put the pan in the air fryer. Cook at 350°F for about 13 minutes. Mix whole milk, butter, brown sugar, and maple syrup in a pan. Boil and continuously stir it. Add in the vanilla extract and pecans. Pour the filling over the crust. Cook in the air fryer for about 12 minutes. Keep in the refrigerator for an hour. Cut into bars when cooled down. Serve and enjoy.

Nutrients: Kcal 414, Fats: 27g, Total Carbs: 42g, Proteins: 4g

9. Peach Cobbler Bites

Prep time: 10 minutes

Cook time: 8 minutes

Servings: 2

Ingredients

- Salt
- 1 peach
- 1/4 cup of egg whites
- 1/4 tsp of vanilla extract
- 1/4 cup of breadcrumbs
- 1 pack of natural sweetener
- 1/4 tsp of cinnamon

Instructions

Cut peach into equal slices. Mix salt, sweetener, cinnamon, and breadcrumbs in a bowl. Mix egg and vanilla extract in a separate bowl. Coat peach slices with it. Then, coat in the breadcrumb mix. Spray some oil on the air fryer basket. Put them in the air fryer. Cook at 392°F for about 8 minutes. Enjoy.

Nutrients: Kcal 144, Fats: 0.5g, Total Carbs: 28.5g, Proteins: 6g

10. Raspberry Muffins

Prep time: 10 minutes

Cook time: 15 minutes

Servings: 6

Ingredients

- 1 egg
- 1/8 tsp of salt
- 1 cup of plain flour
- 1/2 cup of raspberries
- 1/2 tbsp of vanilla extract
- 1/3 cup of whole milk
- 1 tsp of baking powder
- 1/2 tsp of orange zest
- 1/3 cup of brown sugar
- 1/2 tsp of vanilla essence
- 2 1/2 tbsp of vegetable oil

Instructions

Mix salt, baking powder, and flour in a bowl. Take a separate bowl and mix brown sugar, milk, egg, vanilla extract, and vegetable oil in it. Mix both the mixtures.

Then, add in the raspberries. Add the batter to muffin cups sprinkle powdered brown sugar on top. Cook in the air fryer at 375°F for about 15 minutes. Serve and enjoy.

Nutrients: Kcal 196, Fats: 7g, Total Carbs: 29g, Proteins: 3g

11. Air Fried Cinnamon Apple Bites

Prep time: 10 minutes

Cook time: 20 minutes

Servings: 2

Ingredients

- 2 apples
- 1/2 tsp of cinnamon
- 3 tbsp of pecan nuts
- 1 tbsp of maple syrup
- 2 tbsp of cream cheese

Instructions

Preheat the air fryer at 340°F. Cut apple into small pieces. Add cream cheese to apples. Add the pecans and cinnamon over the top. Pour the maple syrup over apple bites. Air fry them for about 20 minutes. Serve and enjoy.

Nutrients: Kcal 276, Fats: 16g, Total Carbs: 35g, Proteins: 3g

12. Grilled Peaches

Prep time: 10 minutes

Cook time: 10 minutes

Servings: 8

Ingredients

- 4 peaches
- 1 tsp of cinnamon
- 2 tbsp of brown sugar
- 2 tbsp of olive oil
- 1/2 cup of unsalted butter

Instructions

Preheat the air fryer at 350°F. Mix cinnamon, brown sugar, and butter in a bowl. Set it aside. Cut peaches into pieces. Spray olive oil over pieces and place it in the air fryer basket. Cook for about 10 minutes on each side. Serve it with ice cream and enjoy.

Nutrition: Kcal 230, Fats: 17g, Total Carbs: 18g, Proteins: 2g

13. Brown Sugar Pizookie

Prep time: 15 minutes

Cook time: 10 minutes

Servings: 6

Ingredients

- 1 egg
- 1 tsp of vanilla extract
- 1/2 cup of unsalted butter
- 1 1/2 cups of flour
- 1/4 tsp of salt
- 1 cup of brown sugar
- 1 tsp of baking powder

Instructions

Mix brown sugar and butter in a bowl. Then, add egg and vanilla extract to it. Mix salt, baking powder, and flour in another bowl. Preheat the air fryer at 350°F for about 10 minutes. Combine both mixtures to make a dough. Spray some oil on a nonstick pan. Put the dough in the pan. Cook in the air fryer for about 10 minutes. Set aside to cool for 10 minutes. Serve and enjoy.

Nutrition: Kcal 399, Fats: 16g, Total Carbs: 59g, Proteins: 4g

14. Blueberry Muffins

Prep time: 15 minutes

Cook time: 10 minutes

Servings: 10

Ingredients

- 2 eggs
- 3/4 cup of oats
- 1/2 tsp of salt
- 1 cup of blueberries
- 1 cup of whole milk
- 1/2 cup of brown sugar
- 1 tsp of vanilla essence
- 1/2 tsp of cinnamon powder
- 1/4 cup of unsalted butter
- 1 1/2 cups of all-purpose flour
- 1 tbsp of baking powder

Instructions

Add all the dry ingredients to a bowl and mix well. Mix wet ingredients in another bowl. Combine both in a large bowl. Add the blueberries to it. Add batter into muffin cups and place them in the air fryer. Set it at 350°F and cook for about 15 minutes. Take out when cooked and enjoy.

Nutrients: Kcal 121, Fats: 5g, Total Carbs: 13g, Proteins: 3g

15. Peanut Butter Smores

Prep time: 5 minutes

Cook time: 2 minutes

Servings: 2

Ingredients

- 1 cup of peanut butter
- 1 tsp of chocolate paste
- 1 marshmallow
- 2 chocolate graham crackers

Instructions

Preheat the air fryer at 400°F. Put peanut butter on every cracker. Put **chocolate paste** and marshmallow over the top. Cook in the preheated air fryer until marshmallow is slightly softened for about a minute. Enjoy.

Nutrients: Kcal 249, Fats: 8.2g, Total Carbs: 41.8g, Proteins: 3.9g

16. Air Fried Banana Bites

Prep time: 5 minutes

Cook time: 5 minutes

Servings: 2

Ingredients

- 2 bananas
- Avocado oil spray

Instructions

Cut the bananas into equal sizes. Preheat the Ninja air fryer to 375°F. Put the banana bites in the air fryer basket. Spray avocado oil. Cook in the air fryer for about 5 minutes until they get brown. Serve and enjoy.

Nutrients: Kcal 107, Fats: 0.7g, Total Carbs: 27g, Proteins: 1.3g

17. Crispy Strawberry Cookies

Prep time: 5 minutes

Cook time: 10 minutes

Servings: 5

Ingredients

- 6 tbsp of unsalted butter
- 1/4 cup of powdered brown sugar
- 3/4 cup of almond flour
- 1/4 cup of strawberry jam

Instructions

Mix the butter and brown sugar till it gets fluffy. Mix almond flour in it. Roll the dough into the shape of a ball. Let it rest for about 5 minutes. Then divide the dough into equal parts. Place parchment paper in the air fryer basket. Place cookies in the air fryer basket and cook at 330°F for about 10 minutes. Let them cool for some time. Enjoy.

Nutrients: Kcal 282, Fats: 17.6g, Total Carbs: 28.4g, Proteins: 3g

18. Apple Pie Bombs

Prep time: 10 minutes

Cook time: 10 minutes

Servings: 15

Ingredients

- 1 can of biscuits
- 1 cup of apple pie filling
- 3 tsp of ground cinnamon
- 1/2 cup of butter, unsalted
- 3/4 cup of brown sugar

Instructions

Preheat the Ninja air fryer at 350°F for about 5 minutes. Crush the biscuits. Mix everything in a bowl. Roll into balls. Cook in the air fryer for about 8 minutes. In another bowl, mix brown sugar, cinnamon, and melted butter. Dip pie bombs into this mixture. Serve and enjoy.

Nutrients: Kcal 124, Fats: 7g, Total Carbs: 16g, Proteins: 1g

19. Healthy Cinnamon Twists

Prep time: 10 minutes

Cook time: 15 minutes

Servings: 5

Ingredients

- 1 cup of all-purpose flour
- 2 tbsp of butter
- 2/3 cup of Greek yogurt
- 1/8 tsp of table salt
- 2 tsp of ground cinnamon
- 1 tsp of baking powder
- 2 tbsp of brown sugar

Instructions

Mix salt, baking powder, and flour in a bowl. Then, add Greek yogurt and mix until a dough forms.

Roll until smooth dough forms. Cut the dough into equal pieces. Shape the pieces into twists and spray the air fryer basket with cooking oil. Cook at 350°F for about 15 minutes.

Mix butter, brown sugar, and cinnamon in a bowl. Pour over twists. Serve warm and enjoy.

Nutrients: Kcal 105, Fats: 2g, Total Carbs: 16g, Proteins: 5g

20. Sweet Potato Fries

Prep time: 10 minutes

Cook time: 18 minutes

Servings: 4

Ingredients

- 2 tbsp of brown sugar
- 2 sweet potatoes
- 1/2 tsp of cinnamon powder
- 1 tbsp of melted butter

Instructions

Preheat the air fryer at 380°F. Cut sweet potatoes into fries. Coat them with melted butter. Cook in the air fryer for about 18 minutes. Sprinkle brown sugar and cinnamon over them. Serve and enjoy.

Nutrients: Kcal 110, Fats: 4g, Total Carbs: 18g, Proteins: 1g

21. Healthy Pumpkin Bread

Prep time: 15 minutes

Cook time: 40 minutes

Servings: 16

Ingredients

- 3 eggs
- 1 tsp of salt
- 1 tsp of cinnamon powder
- 1 cup of vegetable oil
- 2 tsp of baking soda
- 1 can of pumpkin, puree
- 3 cups of almond flour
- 2 cups of brown sugar
- 1.5 tsp of pumpkin pie spice

Instructions

Preheat the air fryer for about 5 minutes at 330°F. Mix all the wet ingredients in a bowl. Mix dry ones in another bowl. Then, gradually mix both the mixtures to make the batter. Grease pan with cooking spray. Pour mixture in it. Cook for about 35 minutes. When it is done, let it cool before slicing. Enjoy.

Nutrients: Kcal 336, Fats: 11g, Total Carbs: 49g, Proteins: 3g

22. Pumpkin Pie

Prep time: 10 minutes

Cook time: 10 minutes

Servings: 10

Ingredients

- 2 eggs
- 1/2 tsp of sea salt
- 1/2 tsp of ginger
- 1 tsp of cinnamon
- 1/4 tsp of cloves
- 1 can of pumpkin
- 3/4 cup of brown sugar
- 10 mini pie crusts
- 1 can of coconut milk

Instructions

Preheat the air fryer for about 5 minutes at 320°F. Mix all the ingredients in a bowl. Place tins in the air fryer. Pour mixture in them. Cook for about 8 minutes at 320°F. Once done, set aside to cool. Serve and enjoy.

Nutrients: Kcal 66, Fats: 2g, Total Carbs: 10g, Proteins: 2g

23. Apple Pie

Prep time: 10 minutes

Cook time: 13 minutes

Servings: 6

Ingredients

- 1 egg
- 1 tbsp of water
- 1 pie crust
- 1 tsp of apple pie spice
- 1 tsp of cinnamon sugar
- 1/2 tsp of vanilla extract
- 1 cup of apple pie filling

1 1/2 tbsp of caramel sauce

Instructions

Mix apple pie filling, caramel sauce, apple pie spice, and vanilla extract in a bowl. Roll out pie crust. Make circles. Make an egg wash by mixing egg and water. Top circles with the egg wash. Place filling mixture in between each circle. Roll edges to seal them. Set the air fryer to 350°F. Cook pies in it until brown. Top with powdered cinnamon and brown sugar. Serve with caramel sauce and enjoy.

Nutrients: Kcal 189, Fats: 8g, Total Carbs: 26g, Proteins: 3g

24. Air Fried Blueberry Cookies

Prep time: 10 minutes

Cook time: 6 minutes

Servings: 6

Ingredients

1 egg

1 tsp of vanilla extract

1 tbsp of melted butter

1 pack of blueberry muffin mix

Instructions

Mix everything in a bowl. Line the basket with parchment paper. Scoop batter into the air fryer basket. Set the air fryer to 320°F and cook for about 6 minutes. Serve and have a good time.

Nutrients: Kcal 23, Fats: 2g, Total Carbs: 1g, Proteins: 1g

25. Pumpkin Cupcakes

Prep time: 20 minutes

Cook time: 12 minutes

Servings: 10

Ingredients

- 3 eggs
- 1 can of pumpkin puree
- 1/4 tsp of cinnamon
- 1 box of spice cake mix
- 1/2 cup of vegetable oil
- 1 tsp of pumpkin pie spice
- 2 cans of cream cheese

Instructions

Combine all ingredients in a bowl. Line molds with cooking spray and parchment paper. Fill molds full with batter. Place them in the air fryer and cook for about 12 minutes at 320°F. Once done, let them cool. Make the icing by mixing cinnamon and cream cheese. Pour in an icing bag. Keep in the fridge for about 5 minutes. Then top the cupcakes with icing. Serve and enjoy.

Nutrients: Kcal 225, Fats: 10g, Total Carbs: 31g, Proteins: 3g

26. Plum Apple Tarts

Prep time: 10 minutes

Cook time: 8 minutes

Servings: 4

Ingredients

- 2 plums
- 1 apple
- 1 egg
- 1 sheet of puff pastry
- 1 tbsp of lemon juice
- 1 tsp of cinnamon
- 3 tbsp of brown sugar
- 1 tbsp of icing sugar

Instructions

Slice apple and plums. Mix fruits, brown sugar, lemon juice, and cinnamon in a bowl. Cut circles out of pastry sheets. Add filling in the center. Brush egg wash on sides and fold. Set the air fryer to 330°F. Cook these tarts for about 8 minutes. Sprinkle powdered sugar on top. Serve and enjoy.

Nutrients: Kcal 143, Fats: 4g, Total Carbs: 26g, Proteins: 3g

CHAPTER 10:

Dressings & Sauces

1. Tomato Sauce

Prep time: 3 minutes

Cook time: 18 minutes

Servings: 4

Ingredients

- 4 tomatoes - 1 onion
- 1 tsp of basil - 2 cloves of garlic
- 1/4 cup of water
- 1/2 tbsp of oregano
- 2 tbsp of tomato paste
- 1 tsp of brown sugar
- 1 1/2 tbsp of olive oil
- 1/2 tsp of sweet paprika
- Pinch of salt and pepper

Instructions

Preheat the air fryer at 400°F for 3 minutes. Chop the onion, tomatoes and garlic cloves. Put all the ingredients in a small bowl and add olive oil. Then add all the spices and mix well. Pour the mixture into the fryer bucket and stir. Then add tomato paste and water to it. Set the timer to about 18 minutes. Stir the ingredients halfway. Serve with favorite meals and enjoy.

Nutrients: Kcal 149, Fats: 6g, Total Carbs: 25g, Proteins: 2g

2. Cranberry Sauce

Prep time: 5 minutes

Cook time: 25 minutes

Servings: 2

Ingredients

- 1/2 cup of water
- 1/8 tsp of salt
- 1/8 tsp of ground cloves
- 1 3/4 cups of brown sugar
- 1/8 tsp of ground ginger
- 1/2 tsp of ground allspice
- 1 pack of frozen cranberries
- 1/2 tsp of ground cinnamon

Instructions

Combine all the ingredients in a bowl. Transfer into air fryer basket. Cook in the air fryer at 400°F for about 20 minutes. Let it cool, store in the refrigerator.

Nutrients: Kcal 135, Fats: 5g, Total Carbs: 20g, Proteins: 3g

3. Romesco Sauce

Prep time: 5 minutes

Cook time: 15 minutes

Servings: 10

Ingredients

- 1/2 tsp of salt
- 2 garlic cloves
- 1/2 cup of olive oil
- 1 tsp of sweet paprika
- 1/4 tsp of ground pepper

- 1/2 cup of roasted tomatoes
- 2 tbsp of fresh parsley, minced
- 1/2 cup of almonds, toasted
- 1 jar of sweet red peppers, roasted
- 1/2 cup of whole wheat crumbs

Instructions

Add everything in the air fryer basket and cook for about 15 minutes at 350°F. Let it cool and then store in a jar.

Nutrients: Kcal 155, Fats: 10g, Total Carbs: 23g, Proteins: 5g

4. BBQ Sauce

Prep time: 5 minutes

Cook time: 5 minutes

Servings: 4

Ingredients

- 1 tbsp of cornstarch
- 1 cup of soy sauce
- 3/4 cup of brown sugar
- 1 tsp of sesame oil
- 2 tbsp of minced garlic
- 1 tbsp of garlic sauce
- 1 tsp of grated fresh ginger
- 1 tbsp of rice vinegar
- 1 1/2 tsp of ground black pepper

Instructions

Add everything in the air fryer basket and cook for about 15 minutes at 400°F. Let it cool. Serve and enjoy!

Nutrients: Kcal: 219, Fats: 1.3g, Total Carbs: 50g, Proteins: 5g

5. Dipping Sauce

Prep time: 3 minutes

Cook time: 5 minutes - Servings: 8

Ingredients

- 4 tbsp of water
- 1/4 cup of soy sauce
- 2 red chili pepper, crushed
- 1 tbsp of rice vinegar
- 3 tbsp of sliced green onions
- 1 1/2 tbsp of brown sugar
- 1 1/2 tsp of sesame seeds, roasted

Instructions

Combine all the ingredients and pour into the air fryer basket. Cook for about 5 minutes at 300°F. Serve and enjoy!

Nutrients: Kcal: 12, Fats: 0.3g, Total Carbs: 1.7g, Proteins: 0.6g

6. Fried Chicken Sauce

Prep time: 5 minutes

Cook time: 5 minutes

Servings: 4

Ingredients

- 1 tbsp of gochujang paste
- 1 tbsp of honey
- 2 tbsp of rice vinegar - 5 tbsp of water - 3 tbsp of tomato ketchup

Instructions

Combine all the ingredients and pour into the air fryer basket. Cook for about 5 minutes at 300°F. Serve and enjoy.

Nutrients: Kcal: 120, Fats: 0.5g, Total Carbs: 12g, Proteins: 1.2g

7. Dumpling Sauce

Prep time: 5 minutes

Cook time: 5 minutes

Servings: 3

Ingredients

- 1 tbsp of water
- 1 tbsp of soy sauce
- 1 tbsp of rice vinegar
- 1 tsp of sesame oil
- 1/2 tsp of sesame seeds
- 1 tbsp of brown sugar
- Chopped scallions

Instructions

Mix all the ingredients and add into the air fryer basket. Cook for about 5 minutes at 350°F. Enjoy with dumplings.

Nutrients: Kcal: 70, Fats: 5g, Total Carbs: 5g, Proteins: 5g

8. Sesame Sauce

Prep time: 5 minutes

Cook time: 5 minutes

Servings: 4

Ingredients

- 4 tbsp of soy sauce - 1/2 tsp of brown sugar - 2 tbsp of sesame oil
- 2 tbsp of rice vinegar
- 1 tsp of roasted sesame seeds
- 1 finely chopped scallion

Instructions

Mix all the ingredients and add into the air fryer basket. Cook for about 5 minutes at 300°F. Enjoy.

Nutrients: Kcal: 20, Fats: 0.9g, Total Carbs: 10g, Proteins: 2g

9. Chives Soy Sauce

Prep time: 5 minutes

Cook time: 5 minutes

Servings: 5

Ingredients

- 1 bunch of dallae
- Pinch of salt
- Pinch of sesame seeds
- 3 tbsp of soy sauce
- 2 tbsp of honey

Instructions

Mix all the ingredients in a bowl and add them into the air fryer basket. Cook for about 5 minutes at 320°F. Enjoy.

Nutrients: Kcal: 120, Fats: 0.9g, Total Carbs: 1.4g, Proteins: 2g

10. Vegan Mayo Sauce

Prep time: 15 minutes

Cook time: 2 minutes

Servings: 10

Ingredients

- 1/2 cup of aquafaba
- 1 tsp of maple syrup
- 1 1/2 tsp of black pepper
- 2 tsp of chili powder
- 1/2 tsp of sea salt
- 1/2 cup of chili oil

Instructions

Mix all the ingredients in a bowl and add to the air fryer basket. Cook for about 5 minutes at 350°F. Store it in an air tight container.

Nutrients: Kcal: 82, Fats: 9g, Total Carbs: 1g, Proteins: 1g

11. Carrot Sauce

Prep time: 20 minutes

Cook time: 20 minutes

Servings: 10

Ingredients

- 1 tbsp of salt
- 1 tsp of black pepper
- 2 tbsp of olive oil
- 1 red onion, diced
- 2 tbsp of chili powder
- 4 cloves of garlic, minced
- 6 ripe tomatoes, chopped
- 1 tbsp of balsamic vinegar
- 1 cup of white wine
- 1 tsp of Italian seasoning
- 1 cup of carrots, chopped

Instructions

Mix all the ingredients in a bowl and add to the air fryer basket. Cook for about 20 minutes at 530°F. Have it with your favorite pasta.

Nutrients: Kcal: 90, Fats: 8g, Total Carbs: 2g, Proteins: 2g

CHAPTER 11:

Liquid & Pureed Recipes

1. Tomato Soup

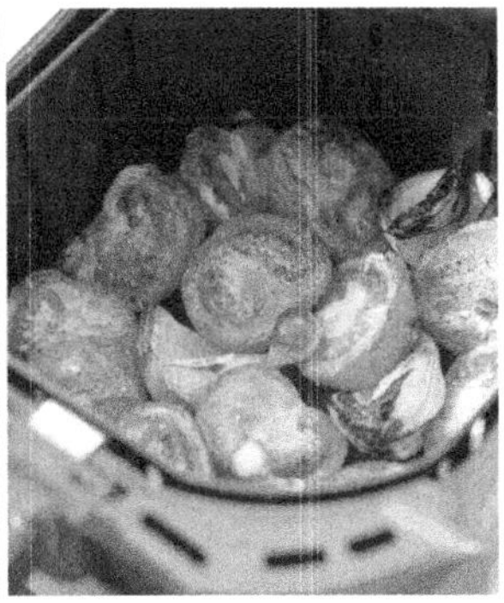

Prep time: 15 minutes

Cook time: 30 minutes

Servings: 6

Ingredients

- 1/2 tsp of salt
- 6 tomatoes, halved
- 1 tsp of garlic powder
- 1 onion, chopped
- 1 tbsp of olive oil
- 5 cloves of garlic, peeled
- 1/4 cup of light cream
- 1/2 tsp of black pepper
- 1 1/2 cups of chicken broth
- 1 tsp of granulated brown sugar
- 1/4 cup of basil, chopped
- 1/4 cup of parmesan cheese, grated

Instructions

Preheat the air fryer to 400°F. To the lined basket, add the tomatoes, garlic cloves and onions. Add brown sugar, salt, olive oil and black pepper to it. Blend all the veggies in a food processor.

Then add chicken broth, garlic powder, light cream and parmesan cheese. Cook for about 30 minutes in the air fryer. Serve with extra cheese and basil.

Nutrients: Kcal: 198, Fats: 7g, Total Carbs: 12g, Proteins: 4g

2. Red Pepper Soup

Prep time: 30 minutes

Cook time: 15 minutes

Servings: 8

Ingredients

- 2 tbsp of olive oil
- 4 red bell peppers
- 4 Scallions, sliced
- 4 tsp of garlic, minced
- 1/2 cup sour cream
- 1 onion, chopped
- 1 1/2 tsp of kosher salt
- 1/4 cup dry white wine
- 1/2 tsp of black pepper
- 4 cups of chicken broth

Instructions

Roast bell peppers. Open the pepper to remove and discard the seeds. Then chop the pepper. Preheat the air fryer to 400°F. Add olive oil, onion, black pepper, garlic and salt. Add everything into the air fryer basket. Cook for about 10 minutes, keep stirring. Then, stir in sour cream.

Puree the soup until smooth. Top with scallions and cilantro.

Nutrients: Kcal: 162, Fats: 7g, Total Carbs: 12g, Proteins: 4g

3. Squash And Butternut Soup

Prep time: 20 minutes

Cook time: 15 minutes

Servings: 4

Ingredients

- Kosher salt
- Black pepper
- Chopped chives
- 3 tbsp of olive oil
- 1/2 cup of heavy cream
- 1/2 onion, chopped
- Roasted pepitas, salted
- 1/2 tsp of ground ginger
- 1 bell pepper, chopped
- 1/4 tsp of dried thyme
- 2 carrots, chopped
- 3/4 tsp of granulated garlic
- 3 cups of vegetable broth, low-sodium
- 1 1/2 lbs of butternut squash, chopped

Instructions

Preheat the air fryer to 375°F. Toss all the ingredients together in a mixing bowl until well combined. Transfer the mixture to the air fryer basket. Cook for about 20 minutes. Then take them out in a bowl. Add broth and heavy cream to blend them in a mixer. Cook the soup in the air fryer for about 5 minutes. Once done, sprinkle pepitas and chives on top. Serve and enjoy.

Nutrients: Kcal: 220, Fats: 7g, Total Carbs: 34g, Proteins: 7g

4. Healthy Bean Soup

Prep time: 30 minutes

Cook time: 20 minutes

Servings: 10

Ingredients

- Cilantro
- 3 tsp of cumin
- 4 tomatoes, diced
- 1/2 cup of water
- 3/4 tsp of sea salt
- 2 jalapenos, diced
- 4 cans of black beans
- 1/4 cup of lime juice
- 1/2 cup of onion, diced
- 2 cups of vegetable broth
- 1/4 cup of cilantro, chopped

Instructions

Mix all the veggies and spices in a bowl. Keep in the fridge for about 30 minutes. Add beans, vegetable broth, cumin, and water in a ramekin.

Cook for about 10 minutes at 400°F. Also, air fry veggies. M

ix everything and cook for 5 minutes. Top with cilantro and serve.

Nutrients: Kcal: 250, Fats: 8g, Total Carbs: 44g, Proteins: 9g

5. Creamy Potatoes

Prep time: 5 minutes

Cook time: 25 minutes

Servings: 4

Ingredients

- 2 tbsp of butter
- 2 stalks of fresh chives
- 1/4 cup of cream cheese
- Salt and pepper to taste
- 2 lbs of baking potatoes

Instructions

Wrap potatoes in foil and place in air fryer basket. Cook for about 25 minutes at 400°F. Once done, mash potatoes.

Add melted butter, chives, and cream cheese to it. Mix well. Serve and enjoy.

Nutrients: Kcal: 332, Fats: 11g, Total Carbs: 50g, Proteins: 7g

6. Cauliflower Mash

Prep time: 10 minutes

Cook time: 25 minutes

Servings: 4

Ingredients

- 3 tbsp of butter
- 1/2 tsp of salt
- 6 slices of bacon
- 1/4 tsp of black pepper
- 1/4 cup of heavy cream
- 1/2 tsp of garlic powder
- 6 cups of cauliflower florets
- 6 ounces of shredded gouda

Instructions

Chop cauliflower into small pieces. Mix everything in a bowl except bacon, cream, and gouda. Place it in the air fryer at 400°F for about 15 minutes. Then blend cauliflower, spices, bacon, butter, and heavy cream in a blender. Sprinkle some parsley and bacon on top of the mixture. Serve and enjoy.

Nutrients: Kcal: 215, Fats: 7g, Total Carbs: 45g, Proteins: 8g

7. Potato Balls

Prep time: 30 minutes

Cook time: 5 minutes

Servings: 25

Ingredients

- 2 eggs - 10 potatoes
- Cooking spray - 10 slices of bacon
- 1 tsp of garlic powder
- 1 tbsp of butter, unsalted
- 3/4 cup of green onion
- 1/4 cup parmesan cheese
- 1 1/2 cups of cheddar cheese
- 1 1/2 cups of breadcrumbs

Instructions

Boil potatoes. Fry bacon pieces in a pan. Shred cheese. Chop onions. Mash boiled potatoes with a fork. Add salt, butter, pepper, and garlic powder to it. Mix well. Then add the bacon, chopped onion, shredded cheese and mash again. Whisk the eggs in a bowl. In another bowl, mix parmesan cheese and breadcrumbs. Make small balls with potato mixture. Dip in egg mixture and then coat with breadcrumbs mixture. Grease air fryer basket with cooking spray. Cook these potato balls in the air fryer for about 5 minutes at 400°F. Serve and enjoy.

Nutrients: Kcal: 115, Fats: 5g, Total Carbs: 7g, Proteins: 3g

8. Mashed Squash

Prep time: 5 minutes

Cook time: 20 minutes

Servings: 2

Ingredients

- Cooking spray
- 2 Butternut squash
- Salt and pepper, as per taste

Instructions

Chop squash. Remove seeds. Place these in the air fryer basket and cook for about 20 minutes at 250°F. Then mash them in a bowl. Add salt and pepper. Serve and enjoy.

Nutrients: Kcal: 105, Fats: 4g, Total Carbs: 8g, Proteins: 5g

CHAPTER 12:

30 Days Meal Plan

Day 1:

- **Breakfast:** Scrambled eggs with whole wheat toast and sliced avocado
- **Snack:** Apple slices with almond butter
- **Lunch:** Grilled chicken salad with mixed greens, cherry tomatoes, and balsamic vinaigrette
- **Snack:** Greek yogurt with mixed berries
- **Dinner:** Baked salmon with roasted asparagus and quinoa

Day 2:

- **Breakfast**: Greek yogurt with granola and sliced banana
- **Snack**: Carrots with hummus
- **Lunch:** Turkey wrap with lettuce, tomato, and mustard
- **Snack:** Trail mix with nuts and dried fruit
- **Dinner**: Grilled steak with roasted sweet potato and green beans

Day 3:

- **Breakfast:** Oatmeal with sliced strawberries and almond milk
- **Snack:** Celery with peanut butter
- **Lunch:** Grilled chicken Caesar salad with whole wheat croutons
- **Snack:** Hard-boiled egg
- **Dinner:** Baked chicken with roasted Brussels sprouts and brown rice

Day 4:

- **Breakfast:** Smoothie with spinach, banana, and almond milk
- **Snack:** String cheese
- **Lunch:** Tuna salad with mixed greens and cucumber
- **Snack:** Fresh fruit salad
- **Dinner:** Baked cod with steamed broccoli and quinoa

Day 5:

- **Breakfast:** Breakfast burrito with scrambled eggs, black beans, and salsa
- **Snack:** Rice cakes with almond butter and banana slices
- **Lunch:** Grilled chicken wrap with lettuce, tomato, and avocado
- **Snack:** Greek yogurt with mixed berries
- **Dinner:** Beef stir-fry with brown rice and mixed vegetables

Day 6:

- **Breakfast**: Protein pancakes with sliced strawberries and maple syrup
- **Snack:** Baby carrots with ranch dressing
- **Lunch:** Greek salad with feta cheese and olives
- **Snack:** Trail mix with nuts and dried fruit
- **Dinner:** Baked chicken with roasted sweet potato and green beans

Day 7:

- **Breakfast:** Scrambled eggs with whole wheat toast and sliced avocado
- **Snack:** Apple slices with almond butter
- **Lunch:** Turkey chili with mixed vegetables
- **Snack:** Fresh fruit salad
- **Dinner:** Grilled salmon with roasted Brussels sprouts and brown rice

Day 8:

- **Breakfast:** Greek yogurt with granola and sliced banana
- **Snack:** Celery with peanut butter
- **Lunch:** Grilled chicken Caesar salad with whole wheat croutons
- **Snack:** Hard-boiled egg
- **Dinner:** Baked chicken with roasted asparagus and quinoa

Day 9:

- **Breakfast:** Smoothie with spinach, banana, and almond milk
- **Snack:** String cheese
- **Lunch**: Tuna salad with mixed greens and cucumber
- **Snack:** Rice cakes with almond butter and banana slices
- **Dinner:** Beef stir-fry with brown rice and mixed vegetables

Day 10:

- **Breakfast:** Oatmeal with sliced strawberries and almond milk
- **Snack:** Carrots with hummus
- **Lunch:** Grilled chicken salad with mixed greens, cherry tomatoes, and balsamic vinaigrette
- **Snack:** Fresh fruit salad
- **Dinner**: Baked salmon with roasted asparagus and quinoa

Day 11:

- **Breakfast:** Breakfast burrito with scrambled eggs, black beans, and salsa
- **Snack:** Trail mix with nuts and dried fruit
- **Lunch:** Turkey wrap with lettuce, tomato, and mustard
- **Snack:** Greek yogurt with mixed berries
- **Dinner:** Grilled steak with roasted sweet potato and green beans

Day 12:

- **Breakfast:** Oatmeal with banana slices and almond butter
- **Snack:** Apple slices with peanut butter
- **Lunch:** Grilled chicken salad with mixed greens, cherry tomatoes, and avocado
- **Snack:** Carrot sticks with hummus
- **Dinner:** Baked salmon with roasted sweet potatoes and broccoli

Day 13:

- **Breakfast:** Greek yogurt with berries and granola
- **Snack:** Hard-boiled egg
- **Lunch:** Tuna salad with mixed greens, cherry tomatoes, and cucumber
- **Snack:** Celery sticks with almond butter
- **Dinner:** Grilled steak with roasted asparagus and cauliflower rice

Day 14:

- **Breakfast:** Smoothie bowl with spinach, banana, and almond milk topped with granola and coconut flakes
- **Snack:** Orange slices
- **Lunch:** Quinoa salad with chickpeas, red bell pepper, and feta cheese
- **Snack:** Trail mix with nuts and dried fruit
- **Dinner:** Baked chicken breast with roasted Brussels sprouts and brown rice

Day 15:

- **Breakfast:** Scrambled eggs with whole wheat toast and sliced tomatoes
- **Snack:** Cottage cheese with sliced peaches
- **Lunch:** Grilled shrimp salad with mixed greens, avocado, and grapefruit
- **Snack**: Rice cakes with almond butter and sliced banana
- **Dinner:** Baked salmon with roasted sweet potatoes and green beans

Day 16:

- **Breakfast:** Overnight oats with almond milk, chia seeds, and sliced almonds
- **Snack:** Apple slices with cheddar cheese
- **Lunch:** Turkey and cheese sandwich on whole wheat bread with carrot sticks
- **Snack:** Roasted almonds
- **Dinner:** Grilled pork chops with roasted Brussels sprouts and quinoa

Day 17:

- **Breakfast:** Greek yogurt with honey and sliced almonds
- **Snack:** Hard-boiled egg
- **Lunch:** Spinach and feta stuffed chicken breast with roasted sweet potatoes
- **Snack:** Baby carrots with ranch dressing
- **Dinner:** Baked tilapia with roasted asparagus and brown rice

Day 18:

- **Breakfast:** Smoothie with spinach, berries, and almond milk
- **Snack:** Orange slices
- **Lunch:** Chickpea and vegetable stir-fry with brown rice
- **Snack:** Apple slices with peanut butter
- **Dinner**: Grilled chicken skewers with mixed grilled vegetables

Day 19:

- **Breakfast**: Avocado toast with sliced tomatoes and hard-boiled egg
- **Snack**: Trail mix with nuts and dried fruit
- **Lunch**: Tuna salad with mixed greens and cucumber
- **Snack**: Carrot sticks with hummus
- **Dinner**: Baked salmon with roasted broccoli and quinoa

Day 20:

- **Breakfast**: Scrambled eggs with sliced avocado and whole wheat toast
- **Snack**: Cottage cheese with sliced peaches
- **Lunch**: Grilled chicken salad with mixed greens, cherry tomatoes, and avocado
- **Snack**: Rice cakes with almond butter and sliced banana
- **Dinner**: Grilled steak with roasted asparagus and cauliflower rice

Day 21:

- **Breakfast**: Smoothie bowl with spinach, banana, and almond milk topped with granola and coconut flakes
- **Snack**: Baby carrots with ranch dressing
- **Lunch**: Quinoa salad with chickpeas, red bell pepper, and feta cheese
- **Snack**: Hard-boiled egg
- **Dinner**: Baked chicken breast with roasted Brussels sprouts and brown rice

Day 22:

- **Breakfast**: Greek yogurt with honey and mixed berries, whole grain toast
- **Snack**: Carrot sticks with hummus
- **Lunch**: Grilled chicken salad with mixed greens, avocado, cherry tomatoes, and balsamic vinaigrette
- **Snack**: Apple slices with almond butter
- **Dinner**: Baked salmon with roasted Brussels sprouts and sweet potato wedges

Day 23:

- **Breakfast**: Spinach and feta omelette, whole grain toast
- **Snack**: Trail mix with nuts and dried fruit
- **Lunch**: Quinoa and black bean bowl with diced avocado and salsa
- **Snack**: Cottage cheese with sliced peaches
- **Dinner**: Beef stir-fry with mixed vegetables and brown rice

Day 24:

- **Breakfast**: Overnight oats with banana, almond milk, and cinnamon
- **Snack**: String cheese with whole grain crackers
- **Lunch**: Turkey and cheese wrap with lettuce, tomato, and mustard
- **Snack**: Greek yogurt with granola and mixed berries
- **Dinner**: Grilled shrimp skewers with roasted asparagus and quinoa

Day 25:

- **Breakfast**: Veggie and cheese omelette, whole grain toast
- **Snack**: Edamame beans
- **Lunch**: Lentil soup with whole grain crackers and baby carrots
- **Snack**: Apple slices with cheddar cheese
- **Dinner**: Baked chicken with roasted sweet potatoes and green beans

Day 26:

- **Breakfast**: Greek yogurt with honey and mixed berries, whole grain toast
- **Snack**: Carrot sticks with hummus
- **Lunch**: Grilled chicken salad with mixed greens, avocado, cherry tomatoes, and balsamic vinaigrette
- **Snack**: Trail mix with nuts and dried fruit
- **Dinner**: Vegetarian chili with cornbread

Day 27:

- **Breakfast**: Spinach and feta omelette, whole grain toast
- **Snack**: Cottage cheese with sliced peaches
- **Lunch**: Tuna salad with mixed greens, cucumber, and cherry tomatoes
- **Snack**: Apple slices with almond butter
- **Dinner**: Baked salmon with roasted asparagus and quinoa

Day 28:

- **Breakfast**: Overnight oats with banana, almond milk, and cinnamon
- **Snack**: String cheese with baby carrots
- **Lunch**: Grilled chicken wrap with lettuce, tomato, and honey mustard
- **Snack**: Greek yogurt with granola and mixed berries
- **Dinner**: Beef and broccoli stir-fry with brown rice

Day 29:

- **Breakfast**: Veggie and cheese omelette, whole grain toast
- **Snack**: Edamame beans
- **Lunch**: Minestrone soup with whole grain crackers and mixed fruit
- **Snack**: String cheese with whole grain crackers
- **Dinner**: Baked chicken with roasted sweet potatoes and green beans

Day 30:

- **Breakfast**: Greek yogurt with honey and mixed berries, whole grain toast
- **Snack**: Carrot sticks with hummus
- **Lunch**: Grilled shrimp salad with mixed greens, cucumber, and cherry tomatoes
- **Snack**: Apple slices with cheddar cheese
- **Dinner**: Vegetarian stuffed peppers with quinoa and mixed vegetables

Note: This meal plan is just an example and can be modified based on individual preferences and dietary restrictions.

Conclusion

In addition to being an illness that is difficult to treat, obesity also appears to be associated with several other health issues. Its treatment entails more than just a fast diet or surgical procedure. Bariatric patients can anticipate adopting a new way of life that incorporates healthy eating, physical activity, and regular visits to their healthcare providers. This method will provide the best chance of success in preventing weight regain and the recurrence of medical issues.

Bariatric patients are asked to follow a diet explained to them by the team immediately following surgery. Most patients will begin with a liquid diet for a few weeks, then gradually progress to soft foods and, finally, solid foods. All the information regarding the bariatric diet is explained at the start of this book.

After reading this book, you'll be able to follow a bariatric diet in the best way possible. It is important to drink plenty of fluids immediately after surgery, but it can be challenging. They need to stay hydrated each day to avoid nausea, kidney issues, constipation, and exhaustion during their treatment. They also need to pay attention to how much protein they consume. This will entail concentrating on high-protein diets while avoiding high sugar and starch items. Those who do not consume enough protein may suffer from weakness and muscle atrophy, leading to major complications in the future.

This book has low-fat and nutritious recipes for you. It also has a brief range of healthy dessert and snack recipes. This book enables you to enjoy your favorite foods by substituting unhealthy ingredients with healthy ones. Now you also have a list of vegetarian recipes that will help detox your body. You can also make pureed recipes with the help of this book. Now following a bariatric diet isn't difficult for you. Try making these recipes now.

Made in the USA
Las Vegas, NV
14 November 2023

80772351R00057